The Mother's Answer Book

compiled by Verna Birkey
and Jeanette Turnquist

FLEMING H. REVELL COMPANY
OLD TAPPAN, NEW JERSEY

For information on the Enriched Living Workshops taught by Verna Birkey, write: Enriched Living Workshops, P. O. Box 3039, Kent, WA 98032.

Library of Congress Cataloging in Publication Data

Birkey, Verna.
    The mother's answer book.

    1. Parenting—Miscellanea.   2. Mother and child—
Miscellanea.   I. Turnquist, Jeanette.   II. Title.
HQ755.8.B57   1984   649'.1   83-11232
ISBN 0-8007-5127-2 (pbk.)

Contents

5. Discovering Successful Methods of Training Your Child   93

Mothers give wise answers to:

Foreword

"... teach the young women ... to love their
children."

Titus 2:4 KJV

This is a book about mothers, children, and love. One of
the biggest causes of insecurity for a mother is not knowing
how to communicate love so the child really *feels* loved. Paul
declares in this Titus passage that mothers need to be *taught*
how to love their children.

Loving children involves giving time, attention, and gen-
uine interest. It is dealing lovingly and patiently with special
problems. It is the gradual releasing of a child to more and
more freedom of choice. It is the manner we display in all
our dealings with a child. It is humbling ourselves to admit
we were wrong. It is gently leading the child to assume
more responsibility. It is modeling Jesus Christ, making our
children hungry to go God's way. It is carefully planning
fair limits and patiently and consistently holding to them.
These topics and many more put meat on the bones of this
book.

The Mother's Answer Book is composed of 234 true incidents which mothers share. It is mother sharing with mother over the back fence, over a cup of coffee, or on the telephone, "I did it and it worked. Here—try it." It is not a scholarly thesis. It does not pretend to have all the answers.

The value of these pages is their practical simplicity. It's where we live—quibbles over clothes; invasion of privacy; a kitchen swimming in cereal, milk, and chocolate syrup; wet sheets in the morning; unpleasant moods; angry spirits. It's parents playing with their children—"closet-car" with a toddler, fishing with a teen, catalog window-shopping with an emerging teen, making a unique scrapbook for the middle child or a brown-paper town for a budding truck driver, or having Golden Quarters before bedtime. It is Grandma saying, "I wish I had done it this way. . . ." It is daughter saying, "My mother did . . . and it works for me, too." It's like having Grandma around the corner to run to and ask, "How did *you* do it, Grandma?"

Maybe you don't think of yourself as a creative mother. Some of these ideas, which were born out of an actual crisis or need, will be just what you're looking for. You'll see how human all these mothers are, but how God can take even the weakest, who are committed to Him, and make them strong in His might. You may see yourself again and again. As you become aware of what you're doing *right*, be encouraged. As you see some failures, thank the Lord that you've become aware of a blind spot and trust Him for strength to change (*see* Philippians 4:13).

Each true incident is interesting reading in itself, but don't let your involvement stop with a cursive reading. You will gain the most from the book if you thoughtfully and prayerfully consider the truth behind each story. We have added many *Insights for Parenting*. Other insights, you'll have fun digging out yourself. Remember too that not all methods work for every child and in every circumstance. These are *ideas.* Be discerning and wise in your applications.

Some truths may seem ultrasimple, and you'll be tempted to pass them by. Don't. Stop and ask yourself, *Do I really do that?* or, *Is this something that would build the relationship between my child and me?*

We are asking the Lord to make this book a tool to give mothers more confidence in their roles by adding—in very concrete and practical ways—to their understanding of how "to love their children."

Our deep thanks to each Enriched Living Workshop alumna who has shared in this book. Names, places, and some details have been changed in these incidents to assure anonymity.

The Mother's Answer Book

1

Being Your Child's Good Friend

"This is My commandment, that you love one another, just as I have loved you. . . . I have called you friends, for all things that I have heard from My Father I have made known to you."
John 15:12, 15

Though children need to know their parents are the authority in the home, they also need their friendship. How can parents enhance this friendship relationship?

By respecting the child's desires, tastes, and preferences, and by giving him the privilege of making choices.

By learning to see things from his viewpoint.

By seeking to understand and provide for the needs of his whole person: spirit, body, and soul.

By giving of your time and undivided attention.

By showing interest in his interests—sharing whatever constitutes the child's world.

By planning projects to be done together—alone with each individual child.

By assuring him he can share his problems and not be condemned, but rather supported and helped toward a solution.

Verna Birkey
in *God's Pattern for Enriched Living*,
Volume Two Workshop Syllabus

What has opened up fellowship and communication with your teens?

Magic Moments

I used to treasure those brief free moments in the evening after the dinner mess was cleaned up. They were mine! I snuggled down with a book or a newspaper and closed out the family noise around me. It must have been the Lord who began nudging me in my comfort, because I noticed that frequently my two teenagers would come in and sit while I was reading. Sometimes they would try a little talk. Have you ever tried to talk to someone behind a newspaper?

When I realized what was happening, I tried just sitting down with nothing to read. They would come in, a tentative conversation would start, and—if they could gain my whole attention—they would really open up. What a revelation! I had been praying for time to communicate with my teens, and here it was opening up right in our living room. I followed the Lord's nudging and made myself "available." After a few evenings I felt uncomfortable just sitting and doing nothing, waiting for these "magic moments" to happen. I now see why so many mothers knit, crochet, or embroider—you can be busy and listen at the same time!

The old knitting needles are getting the rust knocked off them, and I've relinquished this time for reading, which I treasured, to make myself available to them. Their years at home will soon be over, and then I can read newspapers by the dozens—uninterrupted!

Insight for Parenting: Ask, *Is there a time when my teenager seems more ready to talk to me? What can I do to make myself available then?*

Opportunity Almost Missed

Number-three son, Arnie, was fifteen years old when he started to pester me to go fishing with him. I kept saying, "Someday." At the time I was really concerned about the two older boys and spent most of my time thinking about how to restore communication with them. When Arnie came begging me again with, "Mom, I'll help you—I even have all of the equipment," it suddenly dawned on me that here was a fifteen-year-old boy asking *his mother* to go fishing with him, and she wasn't interested. I had already lost some communication with my older boys. Here was a beautiful way of communicating with this boy, and I had almost missed the opportunity!

You never saw a happier kid when I said I'd go! We bought my five-dollar license, and at 6:00 A.M. the next morning the two of us went to the reservoir. After he showed me how to fix my line and cast, we looked off to the side of the water. A family of ducks came gliding along. Arnie turned to me as I exclaimed my delight at seeing such a treat, "See, you got your five dollars' worth already." I don't particularly like to fish or get up at 5 A.M., but it's worth every minute since I've come to enjoy this boy's company and have the satisfaction of knowing he wants to be with me, too.

Insight for Parenting: Ask, *What is my teenager asking me to do? Have I ever said yes?*

Right to Disagree

In a silly little ceremonious way, I told my emerging teenagers that I wanted to give them something—the right to disagree with me. Now that they're grown, they have reminded me how much this simple little statement helped in our communication during their high school years.

Insight for Parenting: Ask, *Have I given my teens the freedom to begin to become their own person by assuring them I will listen to their side of the issue without rebuke or condemnation?*

What have you done with your toddlers and preschoolers to get to know them and build a good relationship?

Extended Family

My two-year-old daughter loves to look at photos, so we leave several snapshots of her grandparents, uncles, aunts, and cousins around the house where she is able to find them. This allows her to "see" relatives that live out of the area and gives us an opportunity to talk about them and feel closer to them. Sometimes I add photos of our own family doing something together. This lets us talk about places we've been and things we've done together. She asks lots of questions, so it gives us time to talk together as well as keep her aware of the rest of her extended family.

Insight for Parenting: This mother has found a natural way to make scattered relatives more real to her two-year-old. Ask, *In this day of mobile family units, do I take time to introduce my children to their extended family?*

Middle-Child Squeeze

We sensed that our three-year-old son was feeling the "middle-child squeeze." To show him some added love and interest, we helped him make his own scrapbook of his favorite things. We put his picture on the first page, then added pages for each member of the family, our house, and our cat. Together we cut out pictures of his favorite things from magazines—things like toys, food, cars and trucks, and so on. He is thrilled with it and often asks me to "read" to him from his special book. No one else in the family has one like it.

Insight for Parenting: Doing something unique with the middle child can help ease the feeling of "middle-child squeeze."

Closet Car

My little girl loves to sit in her closet and pretend it's her car. She closes the door and tells me, "Bye-bye." Sometimes I try to get "unbusy" long enough to squeeze into her closet, sit on the floor with her, and "go places." You should see her eyes light up! I'm very busy with two babies, but these moments with Lila are precious. When she says, "Let's go bye-bye, Mommy," I try to drop my work and "go places" in the closet!

Make-Believe Mountain

When our two boys were small, quite often on a rainy day we would play make-believe hiking and picnicking in the house. We got our backpacks and prepared them with all we needed for "survival"—Band-Aids, water, first-aid cream, and their favorite sandwiches for lunch. Climbing the stairs to the second floor was "mountain climbing." We climbed slowly, with great grunts and groans, pretending it was a steep climb. Then we'd find a good spot on the "mountain" to sit down and eat our sandwiches. Twenty years later, they fondly recall our make-believe mountain climbing.

Mud Pies and Tea Parties

Before Karen was born, I started saving the caps from cans of hair spray for the sole purpose of giving them to her later to use in making mud pies! The family laughed, but the pile grew quite large and she loves them. We share many tea parties at the table I used as a child, and I adore her, "Sum more?" as she pretends to pour tea into the little cup and passes the plate of imaginary cookies. I don't even mind the discomfort of the nonfitting little chair!

I am so thankful that my husband also feels it is more important for Mommy to "play" with Karen at home rather than take her to a sitter and go to "work." Housekeeping is a joy to me as Karen helps me dust and runs her "popcorn popper" as I run my sweeper. I thrill to every moment of the joys afforded to me as a mother!

Hungry for Knowledge

My three-year-old son is very hungry for knowledge right now, wanting to learn numbers and letters. Quite by accident one morning, I discovered that when baby sister went in for 11 A.M. nap, brother and I could have "school." We do alphabet and pronunciation games, count things, and then have P. E. and he does exercises with me. It is a special time for just the two of us. At this time he calls me "teacher" and I call him "student"—at his request. He feels so grown-up because all the other children in our neighborhood go to school and now he's in "school" too. I am also much more consistent in doing my exercises!

Hurt Sparrow

My four-year-old found a hurt sparrow in the flower bed. It was one of those busy days, but I stopped, got down on my knees beside him, and together we enjoyed his new treasure. We found a box and food for it, you know—the usual procedure. I even took pictures of him holding it. He thought it was great fun to play with Mommy in this unusual way. The bird flew away later that day, but there were moments of special memory left for Mother and son.

Brown-Paper Town

What might have been an ordinary afternoon for my son was changed into a whole new realm of play when I got down on the floor with him and made a "town" with roads, driveways, and cloverleaf expressways on a large piece of paper. The roads were just right for his Matchbox cars to travel on. He made up names for various buildings and homes that he added to the map. When he tired of that "town" several days later, we flipped over the paper and he drew a new one. This project has been repeated at intervals for a year and even interests his older sisters.

Insight for Parenting: A little bit of time and some creative thinking may kick off a mutual activity that will strengthen your ties and enrich your relationship for years to come.

What have you done for a child to draw the two of you closer?

Lunch Special

My son has just started school and likes carrying his lunch. Planning his lunch has become a very special ritual for both of us. "Do we have Joe Mahoney bologna?" has been a frequent question. Or, "May I have five pretzels because I'm five?" Or, "I'd like these seven animal crackers because they are my favorites—Sylvester the Cat, Tweety Bird, Roadrunner, Pepe le Pew, Wile E. Coyote, and two of Speedy Gonzoles." Or, "Those little apples you bought are great!" Most of his requests are reasonable, and I enter into his fun. Before closing his lunch box, I add a short note for him to read at lunch.

Dear Kelly,
Have a good day. I love you very much.
Love, Mom

Love Soap

My nine-year-old son is into soap carving. After I attended Enriched Living and realized I needed to build a stronger relationship with him, I bought two bars of soap

especially for him—a hard kind, good for carving. I put
them on his desk with the following note:

Dear Andy,
I bought these for you because I love you.
Love, Mom.

When he found them, he yelled downstairs, "Thanks,
Mom, for the soap." Later he came to me and said, "Mom,
did you really buy that soap for me? It's not the kind you
usually get."

"Yes, Andy, I put it on my grocery list and picked that
special kind for you because it's hard and good for carving."

His grin and hug and, "Oh, Mom, I love you!" I wouldn't
trade for anything.

Walk and Talk

My two-year-old dominates my time and I feel that I'm
not spending enough with my older son. Last week I asked
him if he wanted to take a walk. As we were walking out the
door he said, "Good, now I can tell you all about what happened today at soccer and in school!" That simple comment
made me realize that he valued time spent with me and that
I'd better make time for more of these walks.

He Felt Left Out

I made clothes for myself and my daughter, but never
thought my son would want to wear "homemade" clothes.
When I discovered that he felt left out and thought I didn't
care as much for him, I made him a shirt. He was so tickled
to receive this shirt made by his mother just for him. He
wore it all the time and would hardly ever take it off—even
to be washed. His love just poured out to me. He would
come up to me saying, "Oh, Mother, I just love you so
much. You're the best mother in the world."

Insight for Parenting: A little bit of time and attention
turns Mother into "the best mother in the world."

Respect, Not Embarrass

My sixth-grade daughter has shown a growing interest in
one special boy ever since the third grade. Her class was
having an outing and needed mothers to help with transpor-
tation. I was willing to drive. It was a delightful surprise to
have this boy share our ride to the outing. However, I was
very much aware how sensitive my daughter would be if I
said anything that might embarrass her. So I respected her
needs, and we all enjoyed our trip very much.

The boy was the last one to leave our car as he carried on
a conversation with me. The most delightful result of this
day was that for the next several nights my daughter and I
had some very special times together—sometimes talking
about God and His Word, sometimes having a "tickle
fight." As I looked back, wondering why the sudden out-
burst of sweet fellowship between us, I recognized that the
beginning was that day when the Lord enabled me to respect her as a person and not embarrass her while driving
her and her special friend to the outing.

Insight for Parenting: This mother's obvious respect
for her daughter's feelings released a new trust and
encouraged a new surge of friendship between them.

Balls and Strikes

My eight-year-old is wild about sports, but I didn't know
the difference between "balls" and "strikes." I started read-

ing the sports section of the newspaper, especially concentrating on learning about the players. When a natural occasion arose, I would mention an article or something I had read about a game or sports figure. At first he was amazed that I knew anything about sports! Now he shares more of his interests with me, not just sports.

Insight for Parenting: Mother's learning something about his interests gave him the desire to share other areas of his life with her.

Commending Words

When each child comes home from school, I try to have a special message for each of them to read. Throughout the day, as I think of things to tell them, I write them down and leave notes in the kitchen. They always run for them as soon as they get in the door. The message may say, "You looked so nice in your yellow sweater today." Or, "Thank you for cleaning out the closet." Or, "I'd like to play a game with you after supper." Or, "I have a new book to read to you tonight."

They are not reminders of jobs, but happy, encouraging, commending words. It starts the evening off on a glad note.

Brown Bag Wins Over Raiders

Nothing was more important to my son than what kind of lunch box he had. As an active third-grade boy, a "Raiders" lunch box was his greatest possession. His sixth-grade sister was not nearly as concerned about such things, so last year six weeks before school was out, when her lunch box broke, she chose to carry a brown bag for the rest of the school year.

To keep her bag from being too plain, I would write notes of praise on the bottom each day. After two days of this as I was making lunches, my son came charging into the kitchen to announce, to my surprise, that he would prefer a bag that day. On the bottom of his bag I put a note of praise and love for him. His Raiders lunch box hasn't been out of the cupboard since. These things that take so little time to do can mean so very much to someone you love.

Insight for Parenting: How hungry children are for words of love and praise! Ask, *What could I write on the bottom of the brown bags tomorrow morning?*

How do you have fun with your kids?

Treasured Togetherness

Occasionally during a heavy rain I take one child to the attic to sit on the floor in the dark and listen to raindrops on the roof. They treasure the togetherness and the mystery of the cozy, dark place. Sometimes we sit silently, listening. Sometimes we talk about God and the wonder of His ways. Sometimes the child wants to talk about things in his little world. But we always come back to the family with a quieter spirit.

Mom's Old Shoes

Recently I noticed my son alone in the backyard catching baseballs with a "pitch-back" device. Although he loves baseball, he was scowling and grumbling and didn't seem to be enjoying this lonely method. I grew up with all brothers and baseball is not foreign to me, so I stopped what I was doing, put on my old shoes, and went out to ask him if he'd like to play catch with me. He broke into a big grin and his eyes began to shine. "Hey, great, Mom!" he replied to my inquiry, as he dashed happily in to get me a mitt.

We spent some time catching as he chattered happily, grinning and giggling at my rusty pitching efforts. Then he volunteered to come inside and set the dinner table while I finished cooking dinner. His chatter and happy mood continued in the kitchen and even right through till bedtime. Occasionally since then, I'll put on my old shoes and my mitt so I can listen to his happy chatter.

Insight for Parenting: These mothers were wise to set up an atmosphere, alone with Mom, where the child felt important and could talk freely.

The Three Bears

One evening recently when my husband was out of town working, my five- and seven-year-olds and I were having frozen chicken pies for dinner. When we sat down to eat, the pies were very hot and the kids were complaining about not being able to eat them. Suddenly I thought of "Goldilocks and the Three Bears." The wonderful world of a child's imagination turned our chicken pies into "porridge" and a mother and her two boys into the Three Bears. We held one another's hands and went for a walk while our "porridge" cooled off. We had a good time pretending Goldilocks might be in the house tasting our dinner. We enjoyed the walk together and when we got back, our chicken pie "porridge" was just right and we ate it all up!

Insight for Parenting: This spur-of-the-moment fun turned a potentially lonely dinner without Dad into a lively world of make-believe. Ask, *Could I use this same idea, or is there another favorite story I could incorporate into our evening meal or activity as a fun time together?*

Current Fads

There's nothing my daughter likes better than to sit down with me and look at clothes in the catalog. She bubbles over with ideas—why she likes this or that outfit, what shoes would match, what blouse she would wear with it, and so on. I join in her enthusiasm, and in the process I learn a lot about the current fads and fancies of the school crowd. Then I can be more patient and understanding about the way she wants to dress. Occasionally I let her choose one or two items to buy. Her choices are often not the same as mine, but she is learning to manage her wardrobe through our catalog times together.

Insight for Parenting: Capitalizing on this preteen's interest in clothes, this mother patiently showed respect for her daughter's tastes, while building a good foundation of communication and understanding for the teen years.

Mother All Mine

Our three daughters are aged five, eight, and nine. Last summer I scheduled one shopping day alone with each girl. The child whose turn it was to go with me could plan the whole day. I asked her which stores she would like to go to, and I was really surprised at things she had noticed before and now wanted to go back and examine more closely. We went leisurely through whatever she wanted to see. I never once said, "Hurry up now." She also got to decide where we would eat lunch. We bought one outfit for the first day of school, and if I took a fancy, I'd buy her something that had really put a sparkle in her eye. We also picked out a small thing for each of the other girls.

The girls were not allowed to compare their trips. I wouldn't tell the others if we had been into this store or that, because the point wasn't to outdo each other. It was valuable to me because of the many things I discovered about my children.

Tina talked the whole time and barely noticed what we ate or saw. She had me all to herself.

Anna hardly talked. She's the middle child and talks all the time at home, but when she was alone with me and didn't need to compete, she was content just to smile at me often and hold my hand. The atmosphere and food were important to her.

Susan is not in school yet and spends lots of time with me, so she tired much sooner because she shops with me all the time.

All of us want to repeat this soon—maybe dinner alone with Mommy and Daddy.

Insight for Parenting: We get to know our children in a new way when they have us all alone for a time. Ask, *How can I spend time alone with each child?*

How has your husband had special times of fellowship with the children?

Biggy, Jiggy, Diddy, Siggy, and Me

I had three brothers and one sister—Billy, John, Daniel, Sally, and I'm Mary Ann. There was the normal amount of vying for attention that goes on in any large family. One way my dad handled this was his famous Squirrel Stories at bedtime as we all sat around on his big bed.

Every night Dad told of the adventurous escapades of five squirrels who lived in the attic. The squirrels' names were Biggy, Jiggy, Diddy, Siggy, and Miggy, but we knew they were squirrel counterparts of us. The best part was that they each had characteristics to match our individual personalities. We could tell before the squirrel's name was even mentioned which one of us Dad was talking about. We sat quietly waiting each night till our squirrel name was finally mentioned. It seemed to provide part of our daily quota of recognition and gave us each a sense of respect for ourselves and one another.

Crack the Code

When my two boys were in high school, I loved volunteering time to their Christian school. One spring I was asked to work on a special project that required long hours each day for six weeks. Feeling overwhelmed with responsibility, I talked it over with my husband. He knew how happy I was, helping at the school, so he asked how he could help me at home so I could complete the six-week project at school. My husband is president of two corporations, serves on several boards, and teaches an adult Sunday school class—a very busy man. When I asked him if he could make lunches for the boys each morning for the next six weeks, the sweetest thing developed. On the outside of the lunch bags where the boys' names would normally be written, he wrote nicknames and endearments, and then began a code such as:

PAGSGTAIWBTTSYLD

Decoded it was: Play a good soccer game today, and I will be there to see you. Love, Dad.

Our boys developed all sorts of friendships at lunch as their friends helped them crack the codes.

Now two years later, one boy is at college, but I'm still volunteering many hours at school, and my dear husband is still packing lunches. In fact, he made *my* lunch today—and I have a code on my lunch bag!

Golden Quarters

For a while in our home my husband gave us all "Golden Quarters" each night. "Golden Quarters" were fifteen-minute segments of time when each of the three children talked and shared with their dad. When they had each had their Golden Quarters, I had mine. They could talk about anything that came to mind, and he would just listen for fifteen minutes. Sometimes he would comment or give advice if they asked, but mainly it was a time of sharing their day with him. The only problem we encountered was that everyone wanted more than fifteen minutes, and the next in line would be waiting eagerly at the door!

Hearts Knit

Every spring when I was a child, my dad and I would choose a Saturday to go to the nursery and pick out flowers and shrubs to be planted around the house. We had loads of fun. This taught me much about plants, plus it gave me special interest in them. It taught me responsibility, because I was in charge of taking care of the plants, but most of all it knit my heart to my dad, and our close, warm relationship deepened and grew as planting time came around each year.

Insight for Parenting: These dads gave a bit of themselves, along with a little time, and communicated a lot of acceptance, recognition, trust, and love.

Enjoyment or Perfection

My husband plays the Autoharp poorly and sings along with it even more poorly. But he loves to sing Christian choruses, and the children love to sing with him because they sense his love of the Lord through his joyous singing. They spend hours together at home learning new Scripture songs, repeating the old familiar ones, and even making up a few tunes of their own for Bible verses they want to learn. It took me a long time to be enthusiastic about their singing because it really isn't harmonious, but now I love it because they enjoy it so, they spend so much time together, and they are learning so much of God's Word.

Insight for Parenting: Remember that enjoying a family activity, even if it is not done with perfection, may be more important than doing the activity with perfection.

What have you done as a family to promote fellowship and togetherness?

What I Learned Today

Almost every night at the supper table, my husband asks our four children and me what new thing we learned that day. It is very interesting and keeps us alert during the day because we know we're going to be asked. He then tells what he has learned. This often relates to something from his morning devotional time and leads into some good discussions.

Mealtime Discussions

In my parents' home we had a nightly ritual that greatly influenced my upbringing. Each night the entire family would gather for the evening meal. After the food was blessed, someone would bring up a particular topic such as a current event, a job or school situation, or a biblical or historical question. That evening we would thoroughly discuss the subject and every family member would enthusiastically interject comments or questions.

It was not uncommon for one or more of us to excuse ourselves from the table and run to get a Bible, a dictionary, an encyclopedia, an atlas, or some other source of information. These discussions often extended one or two hours after the meal. This provided excellent learning experiences in family communication, current events, socializing, companionship, and awareness of our environment, and it was a great educational stimulation.

Insight for Parenting: Ask, *Could we improve our family fellowship during the dinner meal by planning some informal questions or discussion topics?*

Circle for Constructive Criticism

Once a month we all sit on the living room floor in a circle and do the following:

1. We give each child a list of chores for the coming month, trying to make the jobs as equal as possible, considering each child's age and ability. We exchange the chores on the lists each month so the children don't become bored or feel that they always get the "terrible" jobs.

2. We discuss freely what each of us feels about how the others are treating us, or perhaps how we feel we ourselves are failing in some area. For this discussion the rules are: no one can get angry or upset about how the other feels and each one is to have total freedom to share without judgment.

3. We each ask how we can change to be a more pleasant family member. This means taking constructive criticism at an early age.

4. Each of us prays aloud while we all hold hands. We do not leave our circle till we are all "talked out" and understand and accept one another.

Insight for Parenting: Providing a time for everyone to evaluate how he's getting along with the family, gives each person the freedom to share his complaints and helps everyone learn to take constructive criticism.

House Greeting

One good habit I have carried over from my parents' home is that of greeting one another when one enters the house. It's usually a very simple "Hi," or "Hi, Hon," or some other form of endearment, but it creates a feeling of being welcome and belonging to the family. I like to greet my husband at the door with a smile and a readiness to read his mood and take an interest in case he needs a listening ear.

Insight for Parenting: Family members can be made to feel special every time they come or go by some simple greeting. Ask, *Do we show each other we care by saying "Hi," and "Good-bye"?*

Wood Chopping

We decided to burn wood this year because of the rising cost of fuel. This requires many long hours on Saturdays, chopping wood to prepare for winter. I wondered how the children would react to leaving their Saturday morning cartoons. Early on that first day, I packed a picnic lunch, plenty of water, and a small bag of apples. I placed a Laura Ingalls Wilder book in my pocket to read to them when they got tired. We got on our bikes and followed Daddy in the truck to the woods. Even our three-year-old helped load the small logs in the truck, because we were making a game of it. They ate lots of apples and a good lunch. The brisk air and work made us all feel good. Afterward we took a short walk deeper into the woods so Daddy could tell them about trees and birds. We had such a good time, no one even mentioned missing the cartoons.

Grocery Fun

With money and time at such a premium, we have found that grocery shopping can be turned into a family treat. We are busy farm people, and our grocery store is thirty miles away. So we have fun and fellowship and sharing in the car on the way there and, as an extra treat, we eat at an inexpensive restaurant.

Insight for Parenting: Turning the necessary family work into times for fun and fellowship makes for lots of free entertainment.

2

Dealing With a Break in Fellowship

"And be kind to one another, tender-hearted, forgiving each other, just as God in Christ also has forgiven you."

Ephesians 4:32

Weakness, weariness, and sin, never fail to draw forth the deepest sympathy from the Lord Jesus. Nothing lays a stronger hold upon Him, or brings Him more swiftly to our side. At home our mother was always sweet but sweetest when we were ill or weary. It almost tempted us to sham, so as to be more coaxed. And Christ's love is like Mother's. You need not sham with Him, you are weak and broken enough. But those who are most bruised and struggling get the tenderest manifestations of His love. He resembles the strong man, with muscles like iron, and who stands like a rock, but who will bend in tears and tenderness over his cripple-child.

F. B. Meyer
in *Great Verses Through the Bible*

What has caused a break in fellowship
between you and a child?

Not One Harsh Word

When my daughter, Lori, spilled a glass of milk while helping me pick up after dinner, I really did appreciate the way everyone pitched in to clean up the mess. Dad caught the glass before *all* was spilled, Lori grabbed some napkins to keep the drips off the carpet, and brother Bill ran for the wipe-up cloths. Inwardly, I was waiting for Lori to say she was sorry, all the while thinking how nice I was about the whole thing—not one harsh, impatient word from my mouth.

As the minutes went by, my mind kept enlarging her lack of apology. Lori was very quiet through dinner. So was I. I knew she was sorry. I knew also that my irritated, impatient spirit was not hidden by my "nice" exterior reaction. My inner dissatisfaction with Lori's response built a wall between us that communicated rejection.

Insight for Parenting: It's not always the things we *say* that build a wall in our relationships—our spirit can communicate rejection and lack of forgiveness. Ask, *Do I quietly hold inner expectations that grow into irritation?*

Mother Clams Up

We had a house rule never to quarrel during a meal or go to sleep angry with another family member. My daughter remembers one night when I had disapproved of something she did and just said, "I don't want to talk about it." I couldn't recall the incident at all, but she could vividly remember the frustration and confusion she had to take to bed with her. She was especially confused since I had made the "don't-go-to-sleep-mad" rule and then refused to do my part to patch up the problem.

She Pushed to Get In

A secret was one thing my mother never wanted me to have. She wanted to know *everything.* I saw how she treated the secrets of others. "I'm not supposed to share this, but . . . ," so I knew I couldn't trust her. One incident especially stands out in my memory. I had a diary as a teen and I expressed my thoughts quite freely in it. One day as I was reading it over, I found a note from Mother scolding me for what I had written and telling me what an ungrateful daughter I was.

I still can't believe she invaded my privacy like that and then even left a note to reprimand me. I was so angry when I found that note, that I stopped writing in the diary. I made the wall between us even thicker and kept her at a further distance. I needed privacy and the more she pushed to get in, the more I pushed her away.

Insight for Parenting: A thick wall grew as her mother invaded her privacy. Ask, *Do I respect the legitimate privacy of my teens? Have I already begun to show my toddler respect by letting him have things and "places" of his own?*

Phone or Fellowship

When LuAnn comes home from first grade each afternoon, we both enjoy looking over her papers and talking about what went on in school that day. Several times I have received phone calls just before LuAnn came in and unwisely continued the phone conversations after her arrival. I could tell she was disappointed that Mommy was not available to her as usual. By the time I hung up the phone, she was no longer interested in sharing the day's events and there was a definite break in our usual fellowship.

It is so easy to consider a child's sharing of his world as being less important than an adult's sharing his world. I know that if I don't listen to her now, she won't want to talk to me when she is older. I am now making a conscious effort to be off the phone when LuAnn is due to arrive home.

Insight for Parenting: Ask, *Do I talk on the phone too often or at the wrong times for my family's comfort or security?*

"I Promise . . ."

Time and time again I plan special events or make promises to my children and these special promises do not happen at the appointed time. Even though this is often through no fault of mine, the children are left disappointed or perhaps feeling lied to. I am trying not to make promises of *specific* times but instead *possible* times for special treats. I keep to these plans if at all possible, but if it's not possible, we talk about why and make plans for another time.

Insight for Parenting: Keeping promises will tell your child that you are trustworthy and that he is a person of worth.

How has a broken fellowship been mended?

Time Revealed His Hurt

In a moment of anger and frustration I called our son a coward. Immediately I realized my foolishness and told him I was sorry and didn't mean what I had said. However, time revealed how deeply I had hurt him and that time or talk had not erased any of the hurt. Many weeks passed and occasionally a situation would come up that revealed his inner feelings. He felt I really thought he was a coward. I knew my mistake, but I didn't know how to erase *coward* from his mind or how to let our son know I felt he was a wonderful and worthwhile person—*not* a coward.

After praying much about it, I took Ronnie aside and talked with him. I asked him if he'd ever been angry and said something untrue that he really didn't mean. He nodded solemnly. We talked about how we can never erase the words we say. Then I told him how I had done that very thing. I had gotten angry and called him a coward. It wasn't true and I hadn't really believed it, but now I couldn't erase those foolish words. Ronnie understood and we embraced and cried together for a while.

We both learned valuable lessons from this experience, in forgiving and in communicating. Our fellowship was restored, and Mom learned one more lesson in the impor tance of letting the Lord "tame" my tongue (*see* James 3:5–8).

Insight for Parenting: Carelessly speaking a cutting word can sometimes wound so deeply that the memory of it may never be fully erased, but it can be forgiven, the hurt can be healed, and the fellowship can be restored.

He Gave My Dog Away

As we were preparing for a family vacation, my husband didn't know what to do with a small dog we had recently acquired. The dog was a nuisance to him, so he found someone willing to take it and gave it away. Our ten-year-old daughter, Mindy, was heartbroken, but tried hard to conceal it. That caused a breach in our relationship for months, until my husband realized how heartless it was to have given the dog away without discussing it with Mindy or considering her feelings. He realized what he had done, agreed to get a new puppy, and all is well.

Insight for Parenting: Not considering or respecting the feelings of a ten-year-old enough to talk about giving away her dog wounded her spirit and broke the fellowship between her and her father. Ask, *Do I respect my children's feelings, whatever their ages?*

Broken Trust

Rick (twelve years old) has begun to share his thoughts and daily activities when he comes home from school each day. One day we were discussing the profane language some kids use. "And, Mom," he said, "you wouldn't believe the language Mr. Baron (a teacher) used on us today!"

Later that evening, he heard me telling his grandmother over the phone, "Even the teachers are using profane language now. Why, you wouldn't believe. . . !"

Rick got very upset and said, "I'm not going to tell you anything anymore, because you go and tell someone else." I realized then that I had broken a trust with him and our closeness was at stake. After my apology and the promise to keep our conversations private, all was well again, and he still flops down in the old green chair after school and tells me things that are now kept just between the two of us.

Insight for Parenting: Sharing with Grandmother things that he meant only for Mother broke a trust that could only be restored by a sincere apology and a promise to "keep quiet." Ask, *Do I tell everything I hear, or do I realize some things are not for sharing?*

Betrayed Confidence

One of our nephews lived with us for four years while going to high school. His parents were missionaries. After Steve attended camp one summer, he corresponded with a girl he had met there. He was sure it was love at first sight, but all I could think of was my responsibility as his substitute mother. "Would the friendship help or hinder him?" "What kind of a girl was she?" One day while I was cleaning, I saw a letter she had written to him and I read it. He did not know this, but I knew that I had betrayed his confidence in me and that I was wrong.

We always milked the cows together, sharing joys, sorrows, problems, and even confidences at this time. Somehow that night I didn't feel as close to him because of my guilt. So as we sat milking together that evening, I confessed that I had read his private letter and asked his forgiveness. He forgave me quickly and didn't even seem to feel it was a "big thing," but to me it was a relief to get rid of my guilt and have our fellowship restored.

Insight for Parenting: Her guilt built a wall, but her conscience wouldn't let her leave it there. Ask, *Is my conscience sensitive to hear the Holy Spirit's wooings?*

I Was So Upset!

Our preschool son just recently found a bottle of permanent black ink on the road in front of our house. Naturally, out of sheer curiosity he opened it and decided that our front porch needed a new look. Well, it now has a new look. Our white and gray porch is also black polka-dotted!

I was so upset with him. For days I kept reminding him how bad he was. And for days he wouldn't look at anyone. He just hung his head, afraid of what I might say next. When I saw how badly I was hurting him and realized that a new coat of paint would mend the porch, but a little boy's heart was very tender, I stopped picking on him and started forgiving. My little boy has learned his lesson and, I hope, Mommy has learned hers and will keep her mouth shut while she repaints the porch.

My Emotions Took Over

I had spent the whole morning cleaning the kitchen. In two minutes time, while I was upstairs, my two small children had turned it into a total disaster area. One spilled a whole quart of milk across the floor and had chocolate syrup all over the table, while the other one had pulled down a cereal box. I came back just in time to see the cereal soaking into the milk and the chocolate syrup start dripping onto the floor.

That morning I found it hard to actually forgive them for this extra work they made. Both were more than willing to help me clean up, but my own emotions took over and with an angry spirit I sent them both to the living room, while I cleaned up alone.

They both looked so hurt and ashamed. Within minutes my three-year-old came back and said she was sorry for making the mess. She ended with, "I love you, Mommy— very much." My two-year-old put a wet kiss on my cheek. My anger had caused a break in our fellowship, and they couldn't wait to have it restored. The accident was forgiven, and I spent some time instructing them how to get the cereal, the milk, and the chocolate syrup next time.

I Sulked for Several Days

My seven-year-old accidentally broke a rather precious vase. I was so upset at losing the vase, I just tore into him. I sulked about it off and on for several days, and then the incident was gradually forgotten—or I thought it was. Months later Paul woke up as from a bad dream, crying and asking for forgiveness for breaking the vase. How foolish to put such value on a vase and overlook the pain in the heart of a precious child.

My Unpleasant Mood

When I fail to have a forgiving attitude after spanking my preschooler, he will mope around watching me. He knows there's something wrong because of my unpleasant mood.

Although my back is to him, I can feel the presence of a sad, unhappy boy. I can tell him to go into another room, but in a few minutes he will be back, waiting hopefully to be forgiven and received back into fellowship again.

Insight for Parenting: A continuing angry spirit, an unpleasant mood, or constant reference to the offense communicate lack of forgiveness and build a wall of rejection. Ask, *Does it take days for me to truly forgive? What is happening to the child during this time?*

3

Guiding Your Child in the Ways of God

"I have no greater joy than this, to hear of my children walking in the truth."

3 John 4

In your education (of your children), may the coming to Jesus to be saved from sin, to have the heart sanctified and satisfied, be your chief end. Beware of coming between the child and Jesus; let the child under your leading have free access to Him. Beware of hindering him by distrust or coolness. Let the warmth of your love of Jesus, your holy example of obedience, your teaching and praying—in a word, your whole living—be a daily help to the child to see Jesus, to live with Him and to long for Him. Jesus Christ is meant to be our everyday friend, our every-hour companion. Let all the wondrous influence you possess in forming your child . . . be wielded for this one thing: to satisfy the desire of the Savior's heart and to make your child wholly His.

Andrew Murray
in *How to Raise Your Children for Christ*

Share some details of your own or your children's salvation experience that may be helpful to other mothers.

The Bible Was Meaningless

For seventeen years I thought I was a Christian. I had tried to be good, to attend church, and to read the Bible, but it was all rather meaningless. I felt unsettled and never really understood or desired to understand the Bible.

When a friend shared with me that there was nothing I could do to save myself, but that Christ had already done it for me on the cross, I knew that my attempts to be a "good girl" were not what contributed to my salvation. Rather, I needed to acknowledge Christ as Savior and trust Him.

Several nights later I read Romans 5:1–11, and the words began to come alive at last! I read with joy and amazement, "But God demonstrates His own love toward us, in that while we were yet sinners, Christ died for us . . . we shall be saved from the wrath of God through Him . . . we shall be saved by His life . . ." (vv. 8–10). I confessed my sin of trying to be justified before God on my own merit, rather than through Christ, and I asked the Lord to come into my life.

In the weeks that followed, I began to really understand the Scriptures. I read passages that before had been empty words, but now were rich with meaning. Ephesians 2:1–10, Romans 8, and John 14:6 began to make sense to me. I realized that I belonged to the Lord, not by my own merit, but because of who He is, and that I need never again wonder whether I was a Christian. Romans 8:35–39 has fixed that assurance in my heart.

Insight for Parenting: Children need to know that it's not attending church or "being good" that will bring them into a right relationship with God. Ask, *Do each of my children know that Christ died for sinners and that they can be saved through Him?*

Don't Force Me

When Ingrid was in first grade at the Christian school, she came home talking about "accepting Jesus into your heart." As we talked, she seemed confused and uncertain and said, "I don't want to be forced to do it." I felt this was an opportunity to help her understand sin and our need for a Savior, so I used the illustration of disobedience. She understood that. I told her that Jesus' dying on the cross was something like her brother taking a spanking that she deserved.

We talked as long as she seemed to want to, then I said, "Anytime you want to talk about it, I'll be glad to stop what I'm doing, because this is an important decision." Two days later after school she had something very important to tell me. She had decided that this was the day to accept Jesus. We prayed together and she invited Jesus into her heart as tears trickled down her face.

Insight for Parenting: Making sure a child understands the gospel and then trusting the Holy Spirit to convict and convince is better than coercion and pressure. Ask, *Have I opened the door for my child to freely talk with me about spiritual concerns?*

Raised Hand or Cleansed Heart

Our son raised his hand to accept Christ as his Savior during Vacation Bible School at age eight. Several weeks later we were watching an evangelist on television when the Holy Spirit evidently spoke to Kevin. As he prepared for bed, we talked and shared. He told my husband and me that he really didn't accept Christ at V.B.S., but raised his hand only because his cousin and other friends did.

My husband explained the plan of salvation and asked Kevin if he wanted to invite Jesus into his heart at that time. Kevin prayed, receiving Christ into his life. It was our joy to lead our only child to the Lord.

Insight for Parenting: Instead of replying, "But we thought you invited Christ into your heart at V.B.S. last summer," creating confusion and more doubt, these wise parents accepted what the child said and led him at that moment to know Christ as his Savior.

What incidents can you share when "false" assurance of salvation was forced on a child and what were the results?

You Did That, Betsy

As a Sunday school teacher in the primary department, I was talking to the boys and girls about salvation. The invitation was given and Betsy raised her hand. After Sunday school I told her mother about her decision. Her reply was, "Why, Betsy, you did that when you were three years old as you went to bed one night. You're already saved."

Insight for Parenting: How wise this mother would have been to encourage and affirm this new decision and guide Betsy from there to full assurance of salvation instead of bringing confusion to her mind.

No Questions Asked

When I was eight years old, a woman at camp explained how I could become a Christian. She showed me some verses and prayed for me to receive Christ. Without giving me a chance to express myself, ask any questions, or pray, she announced, "Now you are a Christian." No work of God took place in my life that day. I was confused because I had been told, "Now you are a Christian."

For the next sixteen years I lived in the midst of Christians. I knew all the right language. I was even a teacher in a Christian school. Everyone assumed I was a Christian, but my life was characterized by a lack of confidence, a negative, critical spirit, and a fear of the future and death.

Talking with my pastor one day, I finally admitted my doubts. He wisely guided me. I prayed, receiving Christ into my life, and I consider that day the day of my rebirth.

Insight for Parenting: Telling a child he is "now a Christian" without waiting for some sign of understanding on his part usually only confuses him and adds to his lack of assurance.

She Told Me I Was Saved

My mother repeatedly told me how I came to know the Lord when I was four years old. I can't remember a thing about it, but she kept telling me how sure she was that I knew what I was doing. As I grew older I had many doubts, but I was afraid to speak up about them because Mother was so sure. Finally, as a teenager, I made a decision to receive Christ. I look back on that as my point of salvation and I have never doubted again.

Insight for Parenting: It's better to let the child relate the circumstances of his own conversion and not tell it as you think it is. Ask, *Have I provided natural, unpressured opportunities for my child to share his salvation experience with me?*

What problems did you, or someone you know, face in gaining assurance of salvation?

Settling the Doubts

My oldest son received Christ as Savior and was baptized when he was nine. For the next three or four years he would "rededicate" his life about every two months at a church service. Each time, someone in the family would comment that he had "answered the altar call enough to be permanently saved." These comments must have hurt him deeply and certainly didn't help him with his sincere desire for assurance.

I do not know why I allowed the children to be so flip about such a serious matter, or why I never sat down with him and asked him about his doubts. It all came to a head when he was twenty-one and living in his own apartment He called at 2 A.M. and in tears told me he wasn't sure he had ever been saved. I gently told him that he could ask

Jesus to come into his heart right then and settle it once and for all. He did that right there on the phone and has never doubted since.

Insight for Parenting: Being available, without pressure, to seriously discuss spiritual doubts is one of a parent's greatest privileges.

The Questions Plagued Me

When I was seven, an invitation was given on a Sunday morning for anyone who wanted to receive Christ as Savior. I raised my hand and meant it in my heart, but I was afraid to go to the front of the church to have someone talk with me. For years after that, I doubted my salvation. I kept remembering that Sunday morning, but the questions used to plague me, *Was I really saved, even though I did not "go forward"? Was it enough to pray in my seat?*

I went forward many times thereafter for "rededication" of my life, but the doubts concerning salvation did not leave till I was in college. Someone there explained to me that I could accept God's Word as fact. The moment I trusted Him, He forgave. My "position" in my seat or at the front of the church was not important. First John 1:9 became my assurance of God's faithfulness.

Insight for Parenting: It is resting in the facts of the Word of God, rather than feelings, actions, or position that brings assurance of salvation.

Fears

Our son asked Jesus into his heart in Sunday school when he was five. When he was eight, our city experienced an earthquake. This had a very frightening effect on him. For several nights he woke up afraid. After many nights of his getting us up, my husband and I were becoming a bit concerned for him and a bit weary ourselves.

One night when he came in again, my unfeeling response was, "Now what?" Rather than the usual, "I'm afraid," he timidly asked. "Can I ask Jesus into my heart again—just to make sure?" We eagerly replied, "We'll be happy to pray with you again!" After he prayed to receive Christ, we read together 1 John 5:13, "These things I have written to you who believe in the name of the Son of God, in order that you may know that you have eternal life. . . ."

Insight for Parenting: Fear of the earthquake was just a surface problem that brought out this boy's greater need—to know he had eternal life.

God Does Not Lie

I was raised in a home where there was a lot of deception, cover-up, and lies. As far as I was concerned everybody lied—even God. So when I began to hear the gospel, before I could truly believe and receive it, I had to establish in my mind that God does not lie. John 14:2 was a big help. After this was settled I could rest in verses like Acts 2:38 and John 3:16, and I knew I was God's child.

Insight for Parenting: Parents can so easily and unintentionally give their children a faulty concept of God. But God is "bigger" and can draw even such to Himself through the power of His Word. Ask, *By my actions and attitudes do I give my child a true picture of what God is like?*

What methods or timing for family devotions have been successful in your home?

Verse Cards Spark Interest

When we have our personal Bible study, my husband and I choose verses that have special meaning to us. We write them on three-by-five-inch index cards and put them in a recipe file box. On index tabs I have written various categories, for example: Love, Daily Walk, Blessings, Faith, Family, Praise, Honor and Glory, Tragedy, Help With Christ, Prayer, Parents, Temptation, Joy, and so on. We continually add new verses to the box.

At night at family devotions, one child draws out a card and reads the verse aloud. Then we discuss the verse: What does it mean? What is it saying to the family? Does it suggest a prayer we should pray? Since my husband and I have already thought about the verses, we are able to lead the children in meaningful discussion. Often our sparked interest sends us to the Bible to check the context and find even more meaning. That card is then left on the table till morning. At breakfast we see who can remember the verse and share something we talked about. The next night another child reads a card. The whole family looks forward to this.

Insight for Parenting: Variety in family devotional times keeps interest from waning. Ask, *When was the last time I put some effort into making family altar interesting and different?*

Wonder Bag

While my children were ages one through three it seemed important to me to have a short worship in the evening before going to bed. Since I read a lot to them during the day, I wanted a different kind of evening activity. Each week I made up a "Worship Bag." It was nothing more than a large, brown grocery bag, but to the children it was a bag full of wonders! In it I would place small items such as a leaf, a blade of grass, a cotton ball, a feather, a Band-Aid, a pencil, a photo of Grandma, pictures of animals, and so on. The children could pull out one each night and we would discuss how much Jesus shows us His love by giving us these things. At this age they really enjoyed anticipating what would come out of the Bag.

Insight for Parenting: This mother put some wonder and excitement into worship time, giving her preschoolers a happy anticipation for time spent with God.

After-School Bible

This past month our family has been sitting down every day after the kids come home from school and reading from the Bible. We have completed four books of the Bible already. The kids come straight home and eagerly look forward to our Family Time and discussions. It's amazing what a difference this sharing around the Bible has been making in our communications in all other areas. It has unified our family in a way I would not have believed possible. Even twenty-two-month-old Katie shares in holding hands at the opening prayer time. Although she can't read, she has a picture Bible that she knows and recognizes as her own.

Insight for Parenting: This family found that after school was a successful time for their family Bible reading. Ask, *Would we be more consistent in our Bible study if we planned it at another time of day?*

Committed to One Night

My husband is a very busy contractor, but has committed himself to a family Bible study one night a week. He sends each of our teens a letter in the mail stating the study topic and asking specific questions so they are prepared ahead of time. He supplies each with a notebook, dividers, and charts so each child has a neat place to keep all his or her materials. My part is to make that night memorable with good sounds—soft music; good sights—pretty table, clean house; good smells—candles lighted, dinner cooking, good tastes—a favorite dinner each week; and good feelings— hugs for each as they come in the door. I also sit in as a student, not a teacher.

Through this, family life has become critically important to us. Our teenagers have become so open. The rivalry between them is disappearing! And their gratitude to their dad overwhelms us.

Insight for Parenting: This father committed himself to one family altar each week. He keeps his commitment with the same faithfulness as he does important business appointments.

Choose and Read

In making preparation for our vacation, I ask each of the children to choose some stories from their many Bible storybooks. In the morning at our campsite, one will read from the storybook. We each choose one thing from the story to use as our goal or thought for the day. In the evening, as we sit around our camp fire, the other child reads the same story from the Bible and we talk about our goal and how it helped us during the day. The children love the choosing, the reading, the responsibility, and the daily goal.

Insight for Parenting: Letting the children choose and read gave them special enthusiasm.

What are some times and ways you pray together as a family?

Circle of Prayer

A few minutes before our children go off to school in the morning, we gather in a circle with our arms around one another and my husband prays. He thanks the Lord for the kids and prays for their safety to and from school, any tests or projects due that day, and any extra activities. He prays for me, for himself, and for one missionary family. This sounds long, but it actually takes only a couple of minutes. Then we kiss the kids, they kiss us, and we tell each one individually we love them. This seemed to especially help their spirits in going off to school when they were young, but even as teens they still appreciate our routine. It lets them know that the Lord is with them that day, no matter what comes their way.

Insight for Parenting: These parents send their children off in the security of their love and a sense of God's presence. Ask, *Do my children leave home each morning with those two assurances?*

See What We Pray For

We have a "Prayer Board" in our living room. It is a bulletin board on which we put pictures of loved ones and friends for our daughters to pray for. We also add pictures of "things" we need as a family. This allows the girls to "see" what they are praying for, and they have great fun taking down a picture and giving thanks to the Lord when a need has been met. For example, our six-year-old needed shoes and materials for school, so we put up pictures of both. When the prayer was answered, she got to take them down. It teaches us—children *and* parents—to pray for all of our needs, and we are learning that God will answer, no matter how small the need.

Answered Prayer Went Unnoticed

Our family keeps a little notebook on our kitchen table. Each Saturday after breakfast we take time to write prayer requests in it for the upcoming week. Then the requests are

included at grace time before meals. The requests often relate to our activities for the week, but sometimes they are
long-range goals or needs. When the requests are answered,
our youngest daughter has the honor of marking it out after
we thank God for His answer.

Now that we write them down, we are seeing prayers answered. Before this, answered prayer often went unnoticed.
This was my husband's idea, but we all enjoy participating
in writing down the requests and seeing God answer prayer.
One especially wonderful answer was when our little
daughter's kitten was found after being lost for twenty-
one days. She had prayed every day for his return—even
when it looked hopeless.

Insight for Parenting: By these tangible means, the
children see God answering prayer and He becomes
not a faraway God, but close at hand, caring, loving,
and providing. Ask, *Do my children know God like this?*

How have you used "teachable moments" as opportunities for the spiritual training of your children?

Art Treasures

My four-year-old daughter has become a good artist and
quite prolific with her artwork. I used to wait until nap time,
sneak out, and throw away some of the drawings, keeping
the best of the daily stack. Whenever she discovered these
in the trash, it brought howls of objections from daughter
and pangs of guilt for her mother. How could I ever store all
these treasures, much less find the time to look at them
again, until I was old and gray?

Seeing a beautiful picture of a lion she had made one day brought to mind the Scripture about Satan prowling around as a roaring lion, seeking whom he may devour. As I praised her for her artwork, I began to teach her that scriptural truth about Satan. We then decided to write that verse below the picture and do the same thing with other pictures. We now file them in a large loose-leaf notebook, and I read them regularly to my daughter and her friends. The cover proclaims it as "Jana's Own Bible Storybook."

Insight for Parenting: Making an add-on Bible storybook with daughter's artwork gives the family a chance to enjoy her pictures over and over while teaching her Bible truths.

God Answered Prayer

It was a snowy day and I had just taken our baby to the doctor. We had left the clinic and gone to a drive-thru pharmacy to get her medicine. As the man was filling the prescription, our car died. I could feel the pressure mounting within me because the baby was crying, I didn't know how to get the car out of the drive-thru, and I didn't want to take the baby out in the cold again. So I said to our five-year-old son, "I have a very important job for us to do. Please pray with me that our car will start." In a minute I tried again and it started! Our son was so excited. He still remembers this and often talks about how God answered our prayer that day.

Insight for Parenting: Seeing Mother turn to God in the midst of a crisis gave this five-year-old a never-to-be-forgotten lesson in how God answers prayer. Ask, *Do I naturally and quickly turn to God in times of pressure or tension and lead my children to do the same?*

Financially Distressed

Four years ago we were particularly financially distressed and realized we were going to have to depend on God in a new way to provide the things we had previously purchased easily. We started a list called "God's Provision" and recorded everything that came to us free. A friend said, "I think I have a winter coat your daughter can wear." A neighbor offered, "I'm cleaning out my freezer, could you use some chicken parts to make soup?" A relative asked, "Can you come for supper?" (After all, an invitation for supper is also God providing a meal!) And on and on.

As we continued our list, we noticed that when God had given us money, we got less free. Seeing a recorded list makes you realize how much God gives and how real He is.

Insight for Parenting: Specifically noticing everything as coming from God's hand gave this family a new dependence on God for physical needs. Ask, *Do we notice and appreciate all that the Father gives or are we teaching our children that the "paycheck provides for our needs"?*

Eleven-Year-Old Evangelism

My eleven-year-old son had a classmate who was a Dallas Cowboy fan—wore the jersey, knew all the players, and watched all the games. The boy had no religious training in the home. Wanting to share Christ with him, my son and I purchased the *Tom Landry and the Dallas Cowboys* comic book. The book not only presented what he was interested in, but also gave the plan of salvation in a "special chalkboard session."

We prayed for the boy and the right time to give the book. One day my son mentioned, "Hey, Mom, my friend really liked the book I gave him, and so did his brothers!" God had showed the proper timing and the book had been given away! What a blessing to work together with my son to share the gospel with his friend!

Insight for Parenting: Planning together with Mother gave this boy confidence in sharing the gospel with his friend. Ask, *Are there evangelism projects we can do as a family?*

Morning Song

In order to set the atmosphere for the day and to commit my own day to the Lord, I began the day singing, "I Have Decided to Follow Jesus." The children soon joined in. Singing became fun and we added other songs. It focused our attention on God, and my son now sings more spiritual songs and fewer TV jingles! Our older children frequently and spontaneously sing songs of praise to Jesus throughout the day.

Insight for Parenting: Mother (or Father) can have a big influence on the daily atmosphere of the home. Ask, *What kind of atmosphere do I create in my home each morning?*

4

Solving Specific Problems

"And so, as those who have been chosen of God,
holy and beloved, put on a heart of compassion,
kindness, humility, gentleness and patience;
bearing with one another, and forgiving each
other, whoever has a complaint against anyone;
just as the Lord forgave you, so also should you."

Colossians 3:12, 13

The family must be a place where problems are brought
and freely and fairly aired. It is the seat of explanation of
some of life's greatest mysteries. Young minds must feel no
reticence in appealing for help in solving life's first riddles.
The most intelligent light should shine into the lives of the
young from within the walls of a peaceful, cheerful and harmonious home. Kindness, gentleness, patience and a will-
ingness to enter into childish troubles, a readiness to take
part in childish joys, are all cords that bind a child's heart
to the parent. This is the way to follow to find the door to
his heart.

Dr. E. Edmund
in *Every Father's Business*

How have you helped a child conquer a specific fear?

Fear of People

Our ten-year-old son was so afraid of people that he spent almost all of his home time in his room. The school bus stops at our front door, but he would never go out and wait for it with the others, preferring instead to wait in his room till he saw the bus coming and then run out just in time to be the last one on. He had no sense of self-worth and felt rejected by us.

When I realized how I had failed him, I began my job of "reconstruction" by asking his forgiveness for not having been the kind of mother God wanted me to be. Then I prayed for an extra amount of love for this child who needed it so. He had never been a physically loving child, so I had quit trying to touch him. Now once again I began to hug him, toss his hair, kiss him, and play catch with him. In addition I began verbalizing praise of his deeds and trying in every way to build his sense of self-worth. As I checked him in bed at night, I whispered, "I love you," in his ear.

The transformation took place gradually and imperceptibly, but today this same boy dashes right up to his room after school to change clothes so he can run down the street to play hockey or baseball with the boys. He goes out early to wait for the bus and plays catch or tag with his friends while he waits. He spends afternoons with a friend or invites a friend home and spends hours with his pal, building models or playing games. His relationships with his siblings continue to improve. This is the same boy who just a few months before had been a fearful "loner," cold and disinterested in life.

Insight for Parenting: Appropriate physical expressions of love and words of love and praise turned a cold loner into a friendly, happy boy. Ask, *What additional words of love and praise can I give my child?*

Fear of Motorcycles

We lived in a neighborhood where, it seemed, every family had a motorcycle. The roaring noise was a common interruption to our conversation. When our boy was three, he cried every night. Because he seemed so frightened, I took a comfortable chair into his room and sat with him until he fell asleep.

One night upon awaking from a nightmare, he revealed his problem. He thought motorcycles were going to come into his bed. I assured him that motorcycles didn't go into houses. Also, I made up stories about a boy who had his name. The story always ended with the fact that this boy knew that motorcycles didn't go into houses, so he wasn't afraid at night when he heard them roaring around. Soon he got over his fears, slept well, and we didn't need the stories any longer.

Insight for Parenting: Words of explanation and understanding and repeated assurances through the "motorcycle stories" calmed his fears and let him sleep, even though the motorcycles still roared.

Fear of Disharmony

At bedtime my son Ronnie would lie awake with his bedroom door open, waiting to hear if my husband and I were going to have a disagreement. At the Workshop, I realized how my bossy attitude was ripping my family apart. I asked my husband to call the kids into the living room so I could talk with them. I asked their forgiveness for trying to run the house as well as run my husband. They graciously responded. We're learning not to fuss, and Ronnie goes right to sleep.

Insight for Parenting: Knowing his mom and dad were getting along gave Ronnie the security he needed, and he no longer had to wait up to see if his parents were going to fuss.

Fear of the Dark

When our small grandson spent the night with us, he wouldn't go to bed or to sleep. He said he was afraid. "I keep hearing all these strange noises, Grandma." So I cuddled him in my arms while I read him some children's Bible stories. We read the story of David alone at night with his sheep. We saw that David wasn't afraid because he knew God was near him in the dark and all the time. All of a sudden Mickey said, "I can go to bed now and not be afraid." Whenever he spent the night after that, he went right to sleep but always reminded me first that he wasn't afraid.

Insight for Parenting: The closeness of Grandma's arms and the truth of God's Word combined to calm a little boy's fear of the dark.

Fear of Water

Our son wanted to be baptized by immersion, but he was afraid to have his whole head under water. My husband suggested that he practice in the bathtub each night. As we tucked him in bed each night we prayed that God would remove this fear and help him do what he knew God wanted. After about a week he said he was ready and the next Sunday he was baptized. He was nine years old at the time. This really built his confidence in God's ability to help him conquer fear and obey God.

Insight for Parenting: A simple exercise, coupled with prayer, gave this nine-year-old a foundation for trusting God in new fears and challenges.

Fear of New Situations

Since birth our thirteen-year-old daughter has been hesitant to move into new situations. The most recent new situation was her going to junior high school. All during sixth grade she dreaded it. When summer began we each (four children and parents) wrote down some summer goals and specific steps to make sure these were accomplished. Her goal was to get prepared for junior high.

To help her meet her goal we got her involved in track. It was something she loved doing. We thought she could get acquainted with kids from all over town and could have some success in doing something well. Great idea, but . . . . She loved working out, but going to the meets was another story. She wouldn't talk to anyone new and when she realized she had a chance to win, she pulled back. We were confused. I decided to have a talk with her.

As a result of our talk, she and I decided that this summer wasn't the time for competition. She wanted, instead, to go out running with me each morning. We could talk, get in shape (one of *my* goals), and just be together. She and I enjoyed each other that summer. In the course of those months, she gained confidence in herself and in our relationship and that seemed to be what she needed most at the time.

As she entered junior high the only suggestion I made was that she say "hi" first to any familiar face. She tried that and has been having a great time socially! We are amazed at this shy girl's adjustment to this new situation. God gets the glory.

Insight for Parenting: Mom gave time and extra love to this shy thirteen-year-old so she could enter this new situation with a foundation of security at home.

Fear of Leaving Mother

When my daughter went to camp for the first time she went alone and knew no one there. As the time approached she didn't want to go. Knowing this, I bought a tote bag with the words *Special Kid* written all over it. I packed it with some books and other small items I knew she wanted. When it was time to leave her at camp and the tears were about to begin, I pulled out the bag and hugged her. I whispered in her ear that I knew she was feeling scared and alone, but when she felt like that she should look at her bag and remember what I thought of her. I left her smiling. A week later she returned home and had had a great time.

Insight for Parenting: A simple gift to remind her of Mother's love made this girl a willing and happy camper.

What have you done to help eliminate nervous habits such as nail-biting?

Knuckle-Popping

We have a daughter who cracks her knuckles. It upset me from the very first, and of course, I reacted wrongly. I would say in a firm tone of voice, "Don't do that!" Or, "That sounds terrible!" Or, "I can't stand that noise!"

It soon became a habit and she did it more and more. It created tension between us. Every time something upset her, she would pop those knuckles. I felt that she also did it to irritate me. I tried talking with her, hoping to create in her the desire to stop this awful habit. I said, "That's not a pleasant sound to others." Or, "Ladies should not crack their knuckles." I even tried to ignore it—quietly asking God to keep me from reacting in a wrong way. Nothing worked!

During the past few weeks, I have been concentrating on her and her needs. She is thirteen years old and I realize that this is often a difficult time for girls. I am trying to be less critical and to praise her more. I try to do things for her that will help to show her that I really love her. I believe she wants to stop this habit. Sometimes she can go through an entire day without popping her knuckles. When she does, I praise her for it. When she slips and cracks those knuckles, I say nothing. The problem is improving and, I hope, will soon disappear.

Insight for Parenting: When Mother stopped reacting to the habit and started concentrating on helping the child, giving more praise and less criticism, the situation improved. Ask, *Am I reacting in irritation to nervous habits of others rather than concentrating on helping them overcome the habit?*

We Fussed

Kathy bit her nails—we fussed. Then she blinked her eyes—we fussed. Then she raised her eyebrows, and we saw how futile our fussing was. Instead, in her nightly prayers we asked God (in her own words), "Help me get through with this habit." Her prayers, plus outward expression of love from us, freed her from these problems.

Insight for Parenting: Nagging and "fussing" at Kathy only increased the nervous habits, while honest recognition of the habit and prayer with parents helped to free her.

Hair-Twisting, Nail-Biting

Our six-year-old daughter is a very high-strung, compulsive child. This makes her prone to nervous habits such as hair-twisting, nail-biting, carelessness, or clumsiness. I have noticed that the more I point out and dwell on her nervous habits, the worse these become. However, when I spend more time with her, openly express my affection to her, and consciously stop nagging her, she tends to become more relaxed and the nervous habits gradually disappear. I pray that I will learn my lesson once and for all about the destructiveness of nagging and belittling. I need Christ's kind of love to keep from falling into these bad habits again and again.

Insight for Parenting: Affection openly expressed, helped the child relax, and the nervous habits gradually disappeared.

How have you met some of the needs of your child during his first years at school?

Waiting on the Porch

When our son started school this fall, his father and I began the year by sitting on the porch with him as he waited to catch the bus. We would also be waiting on the porch for him to return. As the weeks passed, the weather turned cooler, and other things kept us from being on the porch when he returned from school. We did not realize how much this porch routine had meant to Larry until he began to say, "I don't want to go to school." When we reassured him that we would be home waiting for him, his reply was, "But you won't be on the porch!"

A few days later, he made a poster with all our names on it and said, "Mama, I'm going to put a check by your name every day you're waiting for me on the porch." So I will not get a check mark today, but Daddy will and I'll be sure to be there waiting tomorrow!

Insight for Parenting: Those few minutes on the porch each day seemed insignificant to his parents, but to Larry they said, "We love you and are eager to welcome you home again."

A Love Project

My five-year-old daughter was having a very difficult time walking into her kindergarten classroom each morning. Once she had been there a while she was fine, but those first fifteen or twenty minutes really frightened her. So I designed a "love project" for her to carry out each morning. She was to look for some other child that looked sad or seemed to need help of some kind and try to love him or her by meeting that need. Now she walks into class not thinking of herself or how frightened she is, but rather with her eyes on the needs of others.

Insight for Parenting: Turning her thoughts from her own fears to the needs of others helped her to enjoy those first few minutes of school rather than dread them.

Separation Anxiety

When our first child was ready to enter kindergarten I had what I had heard called "separation anxiety." I felt he was too little to be able to take care of himself without me there with him. It was my problem, not my son's—he was looking forward to school. I didn't want him to be a "mama's baby" so during the summer I asked the Lord to prepare me. He did it so tenderly.

First He pointed me to Matthew 7:11 and the story of how much more the Heavenly Father takes care of us than our earthly father and mother. Also my husband supported me with understanding and didn't ridicule me for feeling so silly. And my son was looking forward to school. If he had dreaded it, it would have been much more difficult for me. So I have sensed God's understanding for my motherly instincts. Now each morning before he goes to school, his little brother and I say a short prayer with him and off he goes—smiling. And I usually do too! I hope I remember this lesson when he is graduating from high school and ready to leave the nest.

Insight for Parenting: Through Scripture, the support of her husband, and morning prayers this wise mother prepared herself for kindergarten separation.

A Whispered Prayer

Our first-grader seemed reluctant to leave on the fourth day of school. The year before when she was in kindergarten I had whispered a prayer in her ear as she walked out the door, and we had followed the same routine the first two days this year. I didn't realize the impact and spiritual security this gave her until this fourth day of school. She neared the door and started to cry. As I knelt, put my arms around her, and asked what was wrong, she said amidst the tears, "You didn't pray with me for two days." In our morning hustle and bustle I had forgotten to pray with her. I apologized and whispered a little prayer. At that she burst into greater tears, hugged me, and I gently coaxed her onto the bus.

Insight for Parenting: The security of her mother's prayer helped this first-grader through her day at school.

"You Can Do It"

This has been the first year that two of our three children have been in an American school. Previously they attended Japanese kindergarten and became fluent in Japanese. Five-year-old Lisa has found the adjustment especially difficult. Her teacher told us she was having a great deal of difficulty learning the alphabet.

As we began spending time each day with her, we found it was true—she just could not seem to remember the names of the letters, even when we tried to teach her only four letters at a time and spent thirty minutes on them. Finally it was my husband who realized the problem was a complete lack of confidence. We began encouraging her and offered a small prize each day she could say the letters right. We encouraged her with words like, "You can do it." "That's right." Three weeks later she had no problem with the alphabet.

Lack of Confidence

Our first-grade son was having difficulty getting his work done at school during the allotted time. Consequently he was very discouraged. His teacher, having exhausted her possible solutions, was very frustrated. After spending two hours each evening at home trying to figure out what he was supposed to do and helping him do it, we were also discouraged and frustrated.

I asked permission to visit the classroom to evaluate the reason for Allan's slowness. As I watched and listened that day, I knew he had the mental ability to do the work, but saw that his lack of confidence kept him from accomplishing it. I felt he would respond favorably to an incentive program, so I chose four or five things that I knew Allan really wanted to do or have—stay up half an hour later, have an extra story read to him, go to a quick hamburger place for supper, fifteen minutes of "catch" with Dad, and so on. We told him that every day he came home without any homework he would get one of these rewards. I wrote a note to the teacher explaining what I planned to do and asked for her cooperation by providing "warm fuzzies" of encouragement for him each day. He really worked hard, was able to complete his work on time, and gained confidence. We only needed to use the reward system for a little over a week.

Insight for Parenting: Discovering that slowness in learning was a result of total lack of confidence gave these parents a starting point to build confidence through warm fuzzies and rewards. Ask, *What warm fuzzies can I pass out to help build confidence in a discouraged, frustrated child?*

"Things I Remembered"

My first-grade daughter was always forgetting her coat, sweater, or lunch box at school. She felt bad later, and we were forever frantically trying to retrieve her things. I knew she needed to learn responsibility for her things so we made a list called, "Things I Took to School Today."

Things I Took to School Today

	Mon.	Tues.	Wed.	Thur.	Fri.
coat	√				
sweater	√				
lunch box	√				
book bag	√				
notes	√				

Each day we checked the things she took and also made a list for her to take with her. When she returned, she couldn't wait to show me all the things she had remembered to bring home. In the section marked "Things I Remembered to Bring Home," I would glue a sequin for each of the things she remembered. She loves the shiny sequins and she hasn't forgotten one thing since.

Things I Remembered to Bring Home

	Mon.	Tues.	Wed.	Thur.	Fri.
coat	⚬				
sweater	⚬				
lunch box	⚬				
book bag	⚬				
notes	⚬				

Insight for Parenting: The charts created a fun way to help her take responsibility to care for her things and eliminated the temptation for nagging.

How did you deal with bed-wetting?

The "Potty" Part Worked

When I learned about making statements about God's love and my love to my four-year-old son just before sleep, I also decided to suggest along with it that he would wake up and go to the bathroom in the night instead of wetting his bed. Each night after prayer and talk and all that goes with the bedtime routine, I'd say something like this, "Honey, you know I love you very much. And Jesus loves you too—very, very much. Have a nice sleep. And if you have to go potty, wake up and go to the bathroom, okay?"

In short, it worked! I know the "potty" part worked, and I trust that the assurances of love have sunk in as well. I still go through the bedtime routine, but I don't have to remind him about the bathroom, just assurances of God's love and my love.

Seven Days Dry

We used a calendar and colored in each night our five-year-old daughter stayed dry. We told her that after she had colored in seven days in a row, she would get a special evening out with her mother or father or both. Immediately she stayed dry seven nights in a row, which proved to her and to us that she can stay dry.

She decided she wanted both of us to spend the evening with her, so we made arrangements for a baby-sitter for our youngest daughter and went out for our night together. We played miniature golf and then went for ice cream. She benefited from being treated "special." We continued coloring her calendar. The problem is not completely solved, but it is much better.

Insight for Parenting: Rewarding the five-year-old with a special night out was a workable incentive to stay dry at night.

Ruffled Pants and Rules

We recently adopted a child who was three and a half and still wearing diapers. New ruffled pants took care of the daytime potty training easily enough, but she still wet at night. This particular child had been raised extremely permissively by her foster family and seemed to almost ask for definite rules. I finally just told her very firmly that she must not wet her bed anymore, that she was a big girl now, that her sisters did not wet their beds, and that we expected her not to. It worked, because I think in some way she realized we really cared what she did and were making her a real part of our family.

Insight for Parenting: The firm suggestion made in love, that she not wet her bed, seemed to give the insecure foster child a sense that her new family really cared.

Something Clicked Deep Inside

As a child I had a strong feeling that my dad favored my younger sister. I had no assurance that he loved me or cared for me, but until recently I didn't connect this with my bedwetting problem. My mother tried everything to help me but seemingly to no avail. One day Dad came home from town with a bottle of medicine and gave it to me, explaining how I was to use it to cure my bed-wetting. I remember, oh, so plainly how something clicked deep inside me, *You mean Daddy does care?* I had taken less than a fourth of that medicine when my bed-wetting was completely cured. I gave the medicine to someone else with bed-wetting problems and somehow it didn't work the same wonders for them. The wonder was that Daddy really did care for me and now I knew it.

I Was Uptight and Frustrated

Both Matt and Peter have a bed-wetting problem. I used to be very upset with them and would draw away from them each morning. After many months of frustration for all of us, I realized this was wrong. One day I began to thank God for each boy and the situation as it touched me, and asked Him to help me learn to respond right. This relieved my frustration and slowly the uptight feeling left. Now I try to wake the boys gently before I go to bed, softly reassuring them of my love. The problem isn't totally resolved, as there are still accidents. However, my attitude is different and I can cope with it better, and I even see some progress as a result.

Insight for Parenting: In each of these instances, more patience, attention, time, understanding, and constant reassurance of love did much to decrease the bed-wetting problems.

How did you ease the pain of divorce for yourself or for your children?

A More Adequate Mother

In order to adjust to my new life as a single parent, I realized the importance of spending time with the Lord every day. I also wanted to instill this desire and habit in my two-year-old daughter. At breakfast we have devotions together. In order for her to remember what we talk about, I place construction paper at her eye level and together we illustrate the verses we read. Now when she gets up in the morning, she grabs her little Bible and comes to the table. She can hardly wait till breakfast is over so she can draw, paste, and glue her picture of "what Jesus has done for her." Each idea is also written under the picture. By doing this, she has learned some of her letters and can recognize the words *Jesus* and *God* in the pictures. Example:

God made the sunshine.

We use her children's picture Bible, to find a picture of the sun and read how God created it. Then by letting her see me pray, she has a desire to "talk to Jesus" every morning. This time together with God has made me feel much more adequate as a single parent and it is one to two hours of consistent time that we spend together every day.

Insight for Parenting: This newly single parent wisely realized her source of strength is in God, and in the process of meeting Him each day she greatly influenced her two-year-old's love for Jesus and the Bible. Ask, *Single or married, am I giving God priority time in my life and home so that I can daily draw my strength from Him?*

Rebellious and Sassy

As a divorced person, I was mother and "father" to four daughters, worked, kept the home, and reared the children. Feeling guilty about divorcing the girls' father, I began to indulge my children too much. Not only did they get "their way," but I put too much emphasis on material things. In response, my children began to be rebellious and sassy.

A brother-in-law kindly pointed out the mistakes I was making, and I realized that you can't show love to your children by giving only material things. I began to give more time to teaching my children God's values and the moral codes by which they should live. I gave more of myself and showed more love and concern for their needs and goals. I became more loving, yet firmly expected my girls to be responsible to me and each other.

Insight for Parenting: Giving of herself and her love was far more important than giving material things or the freedom to choose "their way" that the children thought they wanted.

Visits From Dad: Discipline by Mom

My parents were divorced when I was only four. After that I saw my father only on Saturday afternoons for a few hours. Naturally he came to mean special trips to the zoo, museums, and restaurants; and Mom was the one who got the discipline end of the deal. To show her love and let me know she wasn't all disciplinarian, when I returned from a Saturday visit with Dad, she would plan something special. Occasionally I would find something new waiting for me on my bed. These were often practical things such as needed clothes. Sometimes it was playing a favorite game and making popcorn. What a nice surprise as I came home. This thoughtfulness of hers as I was adjusting to this new type of family relationship was very special and meant as much to me as the various entertainments my father provided.

Insight for Parenting: This mother knew she needed to be more than a disciplinarian, so she found this practical way of expressing love at a time that was difficult for both of them.

Children Miles Away

Since I don't have custody of my children, God has given me an opportunity to minister to them through letters to their home many miles away. In these letters I share Christ by relating the things He did for me when I was their age. I praise them for their faithfulness in writing to me. I praise their penmanship. In one letter I gave one son a spelling lesson. I tell them about the frog I caught in the garden. I took a photo of all my stuffed animals and sent it to them, knowing this would appeal to their sense of humor. I write to each child separately, sending little "surprises" to each one so they can know I see them as individuals and not as a group. Their response has been very positive and a source of great blessing and joy to me.

Insight for Parenting: This mother is making the best of a difficult time and building relationships long-distance by the only method available to her at the moment.

How did you encourage piano practice?

The Responsibility Was Mine

My mother went through the usual problems with me in regard to piano lessons. Finally she established a rule that if I didn't practice, and therefore had a bad lesson, I paid for the lesson. She didn't nag or plead with me, because the responsibility was then mine. I really admire her for the way she handled this and I look back on my piano practice with a good feeling.

Insight for Parenting: Having to pay the consequences of not practicing helped the child feel responsible for practicing.

Forget to Complain

After two years of constant struggle between my mother and me regarding piano practice, I could tell that slowly but surely I was beginning to wear her down. She had tried scoldings, spankings, and threats, but I became more stubborn and rebellious.

One afternoon I forgot to complain about or put off practicing and just went to the piano and began to practice without being told. While I was concentrating on the lesson, my mother quietly came into the room. After I had finished playing, she came up behind me, put her arms around me, and hugged me, as she said, "I just love it when my little girl practices without having to be asked!" Talk about warm fuzzies! I cannot remember having to be reminded again to practice.

Insight for Parenting: A few warm, positive words accomplished what all the scolding, spanking, and threatening had failed to.

One-Finger Pieces

My eight-year-old daughter just started piano lessons so her practice time was centered around very simple one-finger pieces that were not very interesting to her. She was also having trouble getting her timing right. I knew she needed to develop discipline to do things that were not always interesting and she could not always have someone nursing her along, but I also wanted her to enjoy her piano practice time. Occasionally now I spend the last ten minutes of her practice time playing the songs with her. Since I play by ear, I improvise a lot of accompaniment to go with the one-finger pieces. She looks forward to the end of the practice time, her timing improves as she plays with me, and we have an enjoyable island of time together.

Insight for Parenting: The anticipation of those last few
fun minutes with Mother gave the daughter perseverance in the monotony of her practice and helped her
improve in a weak area.

Rules and Choices

Piano practice for my ten-year-old daughter became
more goofing off and complaining than practicing. She was
more interested in going out to play with her friends, and of
course, I did much nagging. Finally I decided there must be
a better way of handling the situation.

I sat down with Susan and told her the rules: She must
have a minimum of thirty minutes "quality" practicing time
per day, but she could choose the time of day for practicing.
If she wanted to get up early and practice before school so
that she would have free time to play after school, that was
fine. But if she waited until after school, then practicing
came before playing. If she goofed off, it would just cut
down on the amount of time for playing outside. In other
words, she was given the responsibility of practicing or if
she didn't, suffering the consequences of her own making.
There has been much improvement in Susan's practicing
and a more pleasant atmosphere around the piano.

Insight for Parenting: Setting the amount of time and
giving her some freedom of choice helped Susan assume some responsibility to live by the rules.

How did you help your family adjust to moving to a new community?

Seeing the Move as God's Will

Recently we moved to the mainland from Hawaii after living there eight years. Our twelve-year-old daughter was very fearful and negative about the move. She didn't even want to discuss it. One evening my husband suggested that together we make out a prayer list, specifying all the things we would like to see happen in order to be assured that God was really in this move and was taking care of us.

Lana took off with the project and expanded it into a long list—all beautifully decorated with space for recording the answers. This list was posted in our dining room for several months, and we prayed daily for one of the items about which we had fears or hesitations. Although all are not answered yet, Lana was able to face the move and recognize it as God's will for our family. Her trust in God has grown, and she can now calmly face the future in our new home.

Insight for Parenting: An honest look at the problems related to the move, along with specific prayer, helped the whole family face their fears and see the move as God's will and for their best.

Facing the Unknowns

We recently moved from a small rural community to Chicago. Our three children are eleven, nine, and five. Of course, most five-year-olds are "hep" to try anything, but Brent and Janie found it more difficult to think of all the unknowns they would face. So amid all the traumas of moving, we made two trips to Chicago beforehand to show them special places of interest to them—their library (inside and out), their community swimming pool, their toy store, their donut shop. This helped them so much to realize that the move was not just Daddy and Mommy, but included each of them, too!

Insight for Parenting: Giving the children a foretaste of their new environment lessened their fear of the unknown.

The Security of Boundaries

When my children are faced with a new environment, such as a move to a new house, or a visit to a new beauty shop with Mother, I try to set boundaries for them at the first contact with that environment. This gives them the security of understanding what is expected of them. For example, before visiting the beauty shop, I describe a little about the shop and tell them where they will sit and what they will be allowed to do while we are there.

In a new home I take the children on a tour of "our yard" and explain how far they may go without asking permission. Because of these advance explanations and the fact that any violations are immediately disciplined, we have had very few problems with wandering or unruly children.

Insight for Parenting: Setting boundaries gave the children security in a new environment.

Before the Van Arrived

When we moved as a family from Minnesota to New York City, we concentrated on the future instead of dwelling on all the things we were leaving behind. Long before the moving van came, we did research at the library on this awesome city God was sending us to and looked forward to seeing specific things there. Without the anticipation of seeing the Statue of Liberty and so on we would have been in despair. This seemed to be a light at the end of the tunnel and sustained us as a family until we felt at home there.

Insight for Parenting: Learning about the new city before the move, gave the whole family anticipation and excitement.

How have you prepared children for the arrival of a new baby?

"Sweet Baby"

When I was pregnant with our second child, I saw another mother very upset and frustrated because her fourteen-month-old was trying to kick the new baby off her lap out of jealousy. Since my first child would be only eighteen months old when our baby came home, this frightened me.

After that, several times a week, Erin and I would look at baby pictures—mostly from baby magazines since there's one on each page! We would talk about how precious and tender babies are. I would say, "Sweet baby," "Soft and gentle," and "Ooh. . . ." Erin would hug the pictures and make the same sounds I was making. When we brought Justin home, Erin was just as sweet to him as she was to the pictures, and she has never shown jealousy to her younger brother.

Insight for Parenting: Talking tenderly to the baby pictures helped older sister learn to treat the tiny newborn baby with gentleness.

Eight Arrows

We have been blessed with a nice-sized family—eight arrows to be exact. Every time I went to the hospital to have a baby we would have a small gift wrapped and ready for each child. On my return home with the new addition, the older children would receive their gift from the new baby. I did not realize how much this meant to the children till I was preparing the gifts from the eighth baby. I asked the four older children whether they minded if they didn't get a present. They said no. David said, "Well I'm not as old as the others and I sure would like a present." We play a game of trying to remember the gift they received with each birth. Praise God none of our children has been jealous of a new baby.

Insight for Parenting: Receiving a gift from the new baby made the older children feel special and became a fun family tradition.

Our Baby

When I was expecting our fourth child, our three children were under four years of age. To make them feel a part of "our new baby" we all went shopping and purchased the clothes necessary to take to the hospital for the baby. Each child picked out one necessary item, such as a blanket, shirt, or gown. We could hear them tell their friends, "I got a shirt for our baby and Mom is going to take it to the hospital." This seemed to be quite successful in helping them to accept the new baby.

A Soft Blanket

From the very beginning of my second pregnancy we knew that we could have a problem with our first child becoming jealous and resentful of his new brother or sister. We talked freely to him about the new baby. We also decided to give our son something special to do to prepare for our new arrival.

Since he loved his "soft blanket" so much, we suggested he get one for his new brother or sister. He was thrilled that he had the responsibility and privilege of getting his "brother" a "soft blanket," and he saved and collected his pennies, nickels, and dimes for about seven months. There has not been one bit of jealousy or resentment. He considers his brother "his baby." He even had fifteen dollars left from his money and he chose to buy "brother" some clothes instead of toys for himself.

Insight for Parenting: Providing needed items for the baby helped the older child look forward to the baby's arrival and diminished the possibilities of jealousy.

5

Discovering Successful Methods of Training Your Child

"Shepherd the flock of God among you, exercising oversight not under compulsion, but voluntarily, according to the will of God; and not for sordid gain, but with eagerness; nor yet as lording it over those allotted to your charge, but proving to be examples to the flock."

1 Peter 5:2, 3

We want the most positive, pleasant, loving relationship we can possibly have with a child. At the same time, we want him to develop self-control and act appropriately to the extent that he is able (considering his age, development, etc.). In order to see these two priceless happenings come to pass, parents must give their child two things. First, give him unconditional love, and give it appropriately. Second, give him loving discipline, that is, training in the most positive way possible. Training by all available means, in such a way that enhances a child's self-esteem and does not demean him or hurt his self-concept. Positive guidance to good behavior is far superior to negative punishment for poor behavior.

But no matter how well we do our jobs as parents, a child will sometimes misbehave. This is inevitable. There are no perfect parents and there is no perfect child.

> Ross Campbell
> in *How to Really Love Your Child*

What has been your experience in setting and enforcing rules?

He Made His Own Rules

When Jim was nine he had a terrible time sitting still in church, and his behavior was annoying to all those around us. He could sit motionless in front of the TV for hours if permitted to, so I knew he was able to control himself. Being disciplined after church by added chores during the next week guaranteed good behavior the next Sunday, but was forgotten by the Sunday after that. He was beginning to hate church.

After one particularly wiggly Sunday, instead of my usual extra chores, I handed him a pencil and sheet of paper and asked him to make a list of good behavior for church. After about a half hour he had produced a very sizeable list, which included such items as "Sit up straight. Don't wiggle. Don't whisper. Don't turn around and make faces at Donald. Don't kick the seat." I asked him what we should do if he broke one of his rules. He suggested that each one be worth five minutes in the corner. This seemed pretty reasonable, so we agreed. For the next couple of Sundays I had him read his list over before going to church. It didn't take many weeks for him to eliminate his distracting behavior entirely.

Insight for Parenting: Older children can effectively work with you to set fair rules for specific situations, and as a result, they often feel more responsible to keep them.

I Needed Some Rules

It had been fifteen years since I had taught four-year-olds in Sunday school. My eyes widened as I saw them kick, punch, and pick on each other. Had children changed that much in fifteen years or had I forgotten something key in a "teacher's touch"?

The second Sunday it was obvious I needed some rules, but I was fearful of setting too many or making them too difficult, because I knew once they were set I had to expect the children to keep them. I kept praying for an answer as I read several books on teaching preschoolers. They all reinforced my need for rules, but none of them made any suggestion as to *what* those rules should be.

Fortunately the pastor's son was in the class. The third Sunday, Mrs. Johnson approached me before class, "I want you to know that I want Timmy to obey in class." Those simple words were the beginning of the Lord's answer to my dilemma. In fact I shared my question with her and found that since she taught the same children on Wednesday evening she had already established three simple rules. (1) Keep your feet on the floor, (2) your hands to yourself, (3) and raise your hand to get permission to talk. I analyzed them: The rules control their feet (no kicking), their hands (no punching), and their mouths (only one person speaking at a time).

Since the children were already well acquainted with the rules from their Wednesday night experience, all I had to do that morning was quietly remind them. They did not turn into angels that day. They still have to be reminded again and again because they are in the process of conforming slowly to the actions these rules expect. But the teacher doesn't need to nag about everything. Now she just watches the feet, the hands, and the mouths and can make gentle reminders along the way as we work together toward our goal of self-control.

Insight for Parenting: A few easy-to-remember rules help both teacher (parent) and children know what is expected and give goals to work toward in the growth-and-training process. Ask, *What simple, well-defined rules would help keep order in my group of children and build individual control into the life of each child?*

No Exceptions

The absolute rules that I never make any exceptions to are the easiest to enforce. For example, I allow no snacks after 4 P.M. This rule has been so strictly adhered to that I now just have to glance up at the clock without even saying a word and all the children know my answer.

Insight for Parenting: Consistency is the key to enforcing rules.

Safety Rules

I have discovered that it is more effective to set the rules you want kept before the rules are necessary. For example, I taught a preschool gym class for one term at school and I set the rules before meeting the children:

1. They were to wear bare feet or sneakers each session.
2. They were not to run ahead on the way to the gym.
3. They were to sit and wait until everyone was ready before playing on the equipment.

Most of this was for safety reasons. Had I made the rules after an accident had occurred it would have been unfortunate. Many of the children tried to bend the rules. For example, girls wanted to wear their leotards because they were too much bother to take off. Since the rules were set, they had to choose between participating without leotards or not participating at all. This worked well and they usually cooperated or submitted to silent observation.

Insight for Parenting: Having a good reason for each rule keeps the number of rules at a minimum and makes them more understandable.

Incomplete Chores

Our children were wasting time in the morning and rushing off to school with chores incomplete. We made a rule: If you don't get up early enough to get your chores done and get ready in the morning, you must be sleepy; the solution is to go to bed a half hour earlier that night. Now they're ready on time every morning.

Insight for Parenting: A logical conclusion inspired a rule which solved the problem of morning lolly-gagging.

Give an example of the importance of the right manner on your part as you train or correct a child.

Spirit of Gentleness

The Lord has shown me that the spirit of gentleness is so important to my family. The very moment I allow frustrations to get to me, I quickly say, "Holy Spirit, I yield to You. Please give me the proper emotion I need now." It also helps to repeat the fruit of the Spirit when I feel myself becoming upset with the children. The Lord has never failed to help me.

Insight for Parenting: If children rebel, it is usually not because we have set rules or put limits on them, but rather because of our manner in enforcing them. Ask, *Is my manner gentle in my interaction with my children?*

Consistency

For months there was an undercurrent of grumbling around the house as the Saturday chores were rather grudgingly done by our three children. If one complained to me enough, I might even do part of her job or tell her she could do it next week. When I realized how much they needed to learn to do their chores regularly, without complaint, I saw that I would have to be more consistent and firm in my expectations and instructions. No more reneging on part of their jobs.

It took a few weeks of consistency on my part, but the grumbling stopped (it didn't do any good anymore), and they now do their chores in a routine way, knowing it is required and free time will follow. They even enjoy telling their friends that they can't play because they have chores to do. I believe this is freedom as taught in Scripture.

Insight for Parenting: Consistency on Mother's part helped the children assume the responsibility and gave them a satisfying freedom to do what they ought to do.

The Hate Look

Our five-year-old foster boy hated everything and everyone. Before he came to us he had never known love, but he had learned to control others with a smug smile and a look of hate on his face or "kill" in his eyes. Every time we said no to him, on would go the face of hate.

I said all the wrong things. "Wipe that smile off; you don't scare me!" But, in fact, he did scare me. It was getting so out of hand that he was controlling me daily. While talking to him in his room one day, his face was telling me, "I hate you." In total frustration I turned to see my face in a mirror. The look on my face scared me! I looked so tired and angry. In desperation I cried inside, *Lord, help me with this child. Give me a tool.* As I looked back into the mirror, it was as though God said, "Put love, happiness, and understanding on your face!" Then I realized that I didn't even know how my own face looked. Maybe this boy didn't either.

Lovingly, I lifted him up so we could see our faces in the mirror. As we both looked at the hate and anger and frustration on our faces, I asked, "Is that how we really feel about each other?" Slowly his face softened and tears came down his cheeks. As I began to smile, the anger and frustration melted and I hugged him to me. We have visited that mirror many times since then to check up on our faces, but praise the Lord now, two years later, that same little boy's face says, "I'm happy—I like you. I even like myself."

Insight for Parenting: Unwittingly, this mother's face was mirroring anger and frustration back to the boy. Ask, *What does my face "say" to my children?*

The Voice Rule

When responding to the needs of three active children and a husband, it's not always my first response to be kind, loving, patient, calm, gentle—and all those other good qualities we long to display. When I am especially tired, distracted, hurried, and have many demands on my time and energies, I find it helpful to remember only one "rule." I'm sure it would be a part of "the law of kindness" in Proverbs 31:26, but I express it this way: Focus on your voice. It must be quiet, slow, light, and sweet.

I find it quite impossible to obey this "voice rule" and still frown, say wrong words, or have impatient reactions. A quiet, slow, light, sweet voice also brings a smile to my face and keeps my body movements controlled.

Insight for Parenting: Keeping her focus on a kind voice helps this mother come across in the right manner as she responds to and gives direction to her family.

Private Correction

My mother never corrected us in front of our friends. Instead she took us aside privately to give us the needed discipline. Because of this we knew that she wasn't just trying to humiliate us in front of others.

Insight for Parenting: Administering discipline in private communicates respect for the person and will encourage a better response.

How have the natural consequences of an action been a good means of encouraging a change of behavior?

Hurry and Eat

As a good mother I wanted my kindergartener well fed. Every day I nagged her to hurry and eat her lunch so we could go to school. To eliminate the nagging, I decided to let her experience the consequences of her own decision to play instead of eat. I set a timer for fifteen minutes and told her that when it goes off she has five more minutes, then she most remove her dishes and get ready to go. She had only two hungry afternoons. It's now working very well, and *she* reminds me to set the timer. Our time together before she leaves is much more pleasant.

Insight for Parenting: It may be harder on Mother than on child to let her suffer the consequences of her own choice, but it's well worth it to see the child take responsibility for her own actions.

The Consequences Hurt

My preschool son loves to run down my neighbor's steep blacktop driveway. I talked to Paul many times about this and explained that if he fell while running it would really hurt to have his arms and legs scraped on the driveway. All my warnings were to no avail, so I knew of no other way than to let him suffer the consequences should he fall. I cringed every time I saw him run down the driveway. Then one day the inevitable happened, and Paul came in screaming and limping and bleeding.

"It sure does hurt, Mommy!" I did not say, "I told you so." I just bandaged him up, gave him little kisses, and asked him to please run down the grass when coming down the hill because I loved him and didn't want him to get hurt again. He really learned that lesson in a way that all my pleading and reminding had failed to teach.

Insight for Parenting: Experiencing the pain of his fall, plus his mother's reminder of how to avoid getting hurt again, showed this preschooler that his best choice for running was on the grass.

Where's Breakfast?

I was nagging my oldest boy too often to do the dishes when it was his turn. One night, instead of nagging, I left the dishes as they were—dirty. Nothing was said. When I got up in the morning, there were no clean dishes for breakfast. When the children came for breakfast at the regular time, there was no breakfast. My oldest son, who is always the hungriest, said, "Hey, where's breakfast?"

I responded quietly, "Oh, there were no clean dishes for breakfast." I said nothing else. The children hurriedly got some cereal and we all left for school. When we all returned after school, I sat down to read. Quietly Max, my oldest, went into the kitchen and began the dishes. When he finished, I got up and began dinner. I have not had to remind him to do the dishes since then.

Insight for Parenting: In many areas, natural consequences will teach their own lesson. Sometimes it does away with nagging and works toward a peaceful environment.

Unwise Choices

My parents never disciplined us for making an unwise choice if we came to them to share it. Not having followed their advice and thus having some unwelcome consequences to deal with was "punishment" enough. Because I would be met by understanding and not blame, I always felt that I could share with my parents freely without fear of a lecture from them. They, in turn, helped me see and choose from several alternatives in dealing with the unpleasant consequence.

Insight for Parenting: Not being disciplined or lectured for making an unwise choice, encouraged sharing and advice seeking. Ask, *Do I meet my child with understanding or blame when he faces the consequences of an unwise choice?*

What methods of discipline have been effective for you?

Sarcastic Tongue

My thirteen-year-old son had a very smart mouth. My first attempt to squelch this was to try to "whack" him. I say "try," because he is bigger and stronger than I am and it would frustrate me more than him. I had to find something to check this habit, so when he said something sarcastic, I calmly sent him to his room and told him to stay there until I came to him.

The first time he came out four times; I guess he thought I was kidding. Each time he came out, I calmly reminded him he was to stay there and wait for me. Finally he knew I meant business. After a while I went down and explained how his attitude was wrong and had to change. As his mother, I was responsible to God to train him, and if he spoke this way again I would again send him to his room to cool off and consider his words.

In the beginning his response was quiet disdain, but after a while he began to soften and realize he was in the wrong. I'll never forget the day, after one of our episodes, when he came up and put his arms around me and said he was sorry. We have cried and laughed together many times since. That was the beginning of a great relationship.

Insight for Parenting: Calm consistency on the part of this mother showed she meant business and was the key to releasing this boy from a bad attitude habit.

Confetti Cleanup

Last night my twelve-year-old son spent the night with a friend in the neighborhood. This morning I received a call from a neighbor stating that her yard and shrubs had been "decorated" with toilet paper and confetti. She had been told my son was involved. With some irritation she said this was the second occurrence and she was tired of the laborious cleanup job. I murmured some words of sympathy and replied that I would look into the situation.

My son did not admit to doing the decorating job and I couldn't be sure it was he unless he admitted it. So I told him that if he did not do it, he was to go and tell her so; if he did do it, he was to get started cleaning it up. Shortly after, I saw my son and his friend picking up the little bits of wet tissue paper. It took him six hours of a valuable play day to clean up the tiny confetti, but he has not been involved in such an activity since.

Insight for Parenting: Rather than accuse, this mother wisely gave a choice which brought out the truth. Being given the job of cleanup cured the son of future involvement.

Pray for Mom

Whenever a situation arises that may cause conflict between one of my older teenagers and me, I encourage him to go to his room alone and pray for me that God will give me wisdom and insight into his perspective and need. If he feels I have made a wrong decision he may pray that God will show me this and change my heart.

They already know I pray for wisdom regarding them and that I want God's best for them, so this helps them see their responsibility toward the situation and the importance of their prayers for me. So far this has never failed to resolve any conflict or misunderstanding between us.

Insight for Parenting: Because these teens have the basic confidence that Mother wants God's best for them, they're ready to cooperate in praying for her as she considers their requests.

Happiness Is a Choice

We believe in giving fussing children a choice. It works beautifully! For example, "You may be happy or you may go to your rooms." Usually the fussing stops and I haven't had to nag or arbitrate. If the fussing hasn't stopped, I don't have to listen to it because they are each in separate rooms and they eventually calm down.

Missing the Big Deal

A family tradition for us at Thanksgiving time is that Mother prepares the turkey and dressing and Dad and the three girls stuff, tie, and put the turkey in the oven. Helping with the turkey is a "big deal" in our home. One Thanksgiving day my four-year-old would not pick up her toys. I talked to her several times and then finally told her she could not help with the turkey unless her toys were picked up by the time Daddy was ready for her help. She still refused and sat down in the living room, stubbornly holding her head high until the turkey was stuffed. After a while she walked into the kitchen and looked at it in the oven, sat down on the floor and cried and cried. She never missed out on any more "big deals" after that because she knows now that Mother will keep her promise.

Insight for Parenting: Having stated the alternatives (pick up the toys or miss the "big deal"), this mother kept her word and the four-year-old got one more clear lesson in the sad consequences of disobedience and stubbornness.

Dirty Clothes All Over

Our son had developed a terrible habit of leaving his clothes all over his room. Admonitions had not accomplished a thing. I thought it through very carefully before talking anymore to him about it. Then I came up with a plan. I told him that we would get a hamper for his own room, making it easier for him to put away dirty clothes. After that, if I found as many as three garments lying around, we would go through his clothes, and pick out two pants, two shirts, and two sets of underwear and put all the rest of his clothes into the attic for one month. It would be his responsibility to do the extra wash involved in keeping two sets clean and ready to wear. Not only did the problem disappear, but I heard him telling a friend what would happen if he didn't follow through, and he had a real sense of pride as he told him

---

Insight for Parenting: Mother's well-thought-out plan, which she clearly communicated to her son, not only gave him a new sense of responsibility for his clothes and his room, but added to his sense of security in the love of his parents.

She Had Lied

When our elder daughter, Linda, was in fifth grade, her teacher said she had not handed in an assignment. Linda, who was a good and responsible student, said she had done it. The assignment had supposedly been sent to school with a classmate inside a book while Linda was home sick. We checked with the classmate who said there was no assignment in the book. Our family has always operated on trust, expecting honesty in the other person. So I told Linda I believed her, but I could not accuse the classmate or the teacher of lying, so we would have to go to the school and have a meeting of all parties involved to get to the bottom of the matter.

This really brought home to her how far I would go to stick beside her, but she also realized the tragic results of the sin of lying, because she had lied. Amid a river of tears she admitted the lie to me. She had not done the assignment, was ashamed, and was trying to get out of the situation. There was no need for discipline; she was suffering enough. We did go privately to her teacher, and Linda admitted that she had lied and apologized. I was grateful that the teacher was compassionate but firm.

Insight for Parenting: Realizing her daughter had a repentant heart and was already suffering as a result of her wrong, this sensitive mother felt there was no need for added discipline other than the admission and apology.

No Permission, No Bicycle, No Savings

Without obtaining permission, our son Jack used his sister's bicycle to go to the field to change irrigation water. He completed his work at the opposite end of the field and walked home, so the bike was forgotten until later when our daughter missed it. Jack reported he had used it and explained why he had forgotten it. Our first instructions to retrieve it and return it to his sister went unheeded. Later we reminded him to be sure to get it before dark, since it lay beside a well-traveled country road. He again delayed, and by the time he finally went to get it, the bike had been stolen by a passing motorist.

The money he had earned chopping cotton and hoeing weeds was now required to pay for a replacement for his sister's bicycle instead of the big things he had intended to buy. He did not protest the method of discipline because he realized he had used another person's property without the courtesy of asking permission, had been careless about caring for it, and had not promptly obeyed his parents.

Some time earlier he and a friend had continued to play ball indoors, against our permission, until a window was broken. That time also he had had to use his own earned money to purchase a new windowpane and assist his father in replacing it. There was no third offense.

Insight for Parenting: Making restitution after carelessness and disobedience gave this boy a sense of his
own responsibility and was an effective cure for this
carelessness and disobedience.

Self-Will

One of our girls has had a very resistant will. Through the
years, my husband and I have sought God and taken several
steps of action to correct this, but at ten she still continues
with occasional bouts of strong self-will. Several months
ago when her father was out of town, she and I had a "bat-
tle." Finally, at day's end, her emotions and will erupted
and she shouted, "Well, if I'm that bad, kick me out." Immediately, but very calmly, I began crying. I went quickly to
my bedroom to pray that God would break her will and
mend the rift between us. Within fifteen minutes she came
into my room and pleaded with me to quickly spank her to
free her from her guilt.

Insight for Parenting: The obvious grief and concern of
this mother over the child's self-will was one factor in
breaking that self-will.

Cool Off

When one of our preteen boys misbehaves, he is sent to
his room for a five-minute "cool off" period for him and for
me. After this time is up, I go into the room and ask him if
he knows what he did that was wrong. If he doesn't, I explain what the problem is and tell him why it is wrong.

When I am sure that he understands the *why*, then I ask if he understands the discipline involved (whether a spanking, grounding, scolding, or whatever). Then I administer the appropriate discipline. He is then given another five minutes to cry, cool off, or just think. Almost always, when I return he is very willing, without resentment, to accept the discipline, apologize, and pray with me. It is very important after the last five minutes to let him know that I still love him even though he has misbehaved.

Insight for Parenting: For this mother her "cool off" and discussion approach turns discipline into a learning experience and avoids a buildup of anger and resentment.

Number Ten

We have discovered that each child responds best to a specific method of correction, and it's usually different for each one. It took us ten children to figure this out! Our youngest daughter responds best to a short discussion of what we're not pleased with, rather than grounding or withholding a privilege. If we are concerned about something she is doing or not doing, we sit down at an unrushed time and tell her briefly with no threats. She seldom has anything to say but, "Okay," and we almost always see an immediate improvement. She has told us, "I don't mind being corrected—just don't harp at me or remind me over and over."

Insight for Parenting: Following the principle of using the lightest discipline possible for each disobedience, ask, *Are there times when an open discussion of a problem would be the best method of discipline for any of my children?*

How have you dealt with the challenges of sibling rivalry?

Time to Calm Down

Two of my children were often fighting with each other, either verbally or physically. Not always knowing who was to blame, I had them sit in chairs in opposite ends of the room for a specified period of time. By the end of that time, they were calmed down and ready to play nicely. It was good to have it quiet and I didn't have to hold "court" to discover the wrongdoer.

Settling Disputes

With ten children I did not have time to settle every dispute they came running to me with. Even if I took time, it was impossible to judge who was right and wrong when they were both so impassioned. My solution was to have each write out his side of the argument so I could settle it fairly. Usually they settled it themselves long before anything was handed to me.

Insight for Parenting: Giving the children time to think through the argument often calmed them down enough to "settle out of court."

High Level of Friction

With five children arriving in six years, I spent a lot of time settling quarrels. I found myself often irritated about taking time from what I was doing to solve their problems. My irritation sometimes added to the tension instead of bringing the peace I wanted.

I can't remember how the Lord showed me, but I came to realize that my children were more my "job" than my housework, laundry, canning, and so on. So when I heard the level of friction going above what the children could settle on their own, I called them all in and explained that each would be heard one at a time. After each had spoken, I turned to the one who seemed to be the originator and asked him, "Do you think you were entirely right?"

"No, not entirely."

"Are you ready to assume responsibility for that part and ask _____ to forgive you for your wrong part?"

After that they each took turns asking and receiving forgiveness, and peace returned. Sometimes we had to take quite a lot of time, but we stayed at it until all was well.

Insight for Parenting: God has given to mothers matchless opportunities to lead children in developing relationships by helping them solve sibling conflicts and learn to forgive each other. It's worth the time!

Listening to Grievances

Our sons sounded like a broken record. All they seemed to say was, "Mama, he did this to me." I was becoming more and more frustrated trying to resolve their constant little conflicts and accusations, so I worked out a plan. I call both children to me. Each is to be silent while we listen to the other's grievance. As each shares his side, his fault in the matter becomes obvious to him and many times I don't have to make a judgment. They also know now that I will not listen to a charge or bad report behind the other's back. We are having fewer "hearings" as they are learning to listen to the other fellow's side and express their feelings to each other without involving Mother.

Insight for Parenting: Learning to really listen to each other helped these children to develop their own skills in resolving conflicts. Ask, *Do I listen to childish grievances and take time to help children resolve their own conflicts?*

Undivided Attention

My mom had a special way of treating us when we became angry and hollered at her or one another. She would drop what she was doing and give her undivided attention, quietly saying, "Now if you'll just calm down and repeat that so I can understand what you are saying. . . ." By then we'd be sick of complaining and not bother yelling anymore, or we'd figure out a way of solving the problem without trying to explain it to her. I've tried this with my children and I must confess it works.

Insight for Parenting: Mother's undivided attention, calm spirit, and interest was all they needed to drop their accusations or settle their tiff on their own.

Prayer for Peace

I was peacemaker between our four children with some degree of success. As they became teenagers, rather than enter into a tiff, I quietly took to praying. Usually my attitude of prayer was not obvious to them, but at times they knew I was praying. At first they wondered why I was so quiet and uninvolved and became a bit disgusted with me temporarily because I wasn't helping them toward an agreement. Without me to arbitrate they began resolving their own arguments with the added benefit of Mother's prayers. In time they overcame their disagreements quickly, and I saw God work things out much better than I could have done!

Insight for Parenting: This mother quietly and gradually retreated from her role as peacemaker, putting the responsibility on the teenagers, but helping them toward a solution by her prayers.

If you could start all over, what is one thing you would change in the training of your children?

Less Nagging

I wish I had talked to my children in a more loving way, especially to my daughter. She was messy and sloppy in her room and everything she did. It made me nervous and I nagged her. If I could do it over, I would listen more, nag less, and wait on the Lord daily for His love and patience.

More Calm

I would be more calm during most crises as well as minor incidents. I would remember, "And this too shall pass."

Right, Not Fashionable

I wish I had taught my children what I knew was right—whether or not it was "fashionable" or "in."

Lavish With Praise

I majored on the negative aspects of rearing my children: they were always making messes, constantly interrupting my time, forever slow doing chores, and so forth. They became irritable and unruly, and I was embarrassed by their behavior around other people. They withdrew from sharing with me and decided on their own how to act. I think they must have decided unconsciously to be bad in order to get some kind of attention.

If I could start over I would be more considerate of their normal growth patterns and need for training. I would give explicit instructions on the kind of behavior I expected and I would be lavish with praise and understanding.

Right Reasons for Discipline

I would correct and discipline for disobedience, instead of for things that were irritating to me at the moment.

No Screaming

I would never let my voice get loud enough to be considered a scream. My three-year-old is a screamer, and she learned it from me. I wish I had never screamed at my kids.

A Friend, Not a Teacher

I talked *at* my children, playing the role of teacher. "Do this." "Don't do that." If I could do it over, I would be a friend to each child, discovering them as persons who are fun to be with and developing a deep friendship with each one individually.

Good Reason to Say No

I tend to be a negative person. When my husband or daughter ask for something or want something of me, my first reaction is usually no. Very often I have regretted this. It puts a damper on new ideas and kills enthusiasm. If I could start over, I would try to say, "Let me think about it a moment." This would give me a chance to react logically instead of emotionally. It also gives me time to work out a way to agree or a good, definite reason to say no.

Soft Voice

The nice thing I would do for my loved ones at home is not raise my voice.

Insight for Parenting: Each of these examples carries an obvious insight. Ask, *Is this something I do which I could change now before I have to say, "I wish I had . . ."?*

6

Encouraging Responsibility in Your Child

"It is good for a man that he should bear the yoke in his youth."

Lamentations 3:27

"If you have run with footmen and they have tired you out, then how can you compete with horses? If you fall down in a land of peace, how will you do in the thicket of the Jordan?"

Jeremiah 12:5

What do those verses mean to a parent preparing to release children? If your growing youngster can't cut it at home in such things as cleaning up his room, making his bed, and earning part of his own way by the time of maturity, what on earth will he do when he faces a business career and marriage and the pressures of life? It is good, profitable, healthy, and right for a man to carry some responsibility during his growing-up years. In other words, a key role of the parent is to stretch the child, to challenge him so when he gets to the hard places alone, he knows what it's like to hang in there.

> Charles R. Swindoll
> in *You and Your Child*

What opportunities have you taken to release your child to take more responsibility on his own?

Choosing Outfits

My three-year-old daughter decided she was capable of choosing her own clothes each day. Since I wanted to teach her how to coordinate her clothes while she had "favorites" regardless of compatibility, I devised a solution that was mutually acceptable to both of us. In putting the clean clothes in drawers I folded together a pair of pants and a T-shirt that went with it. Jumpers were hung with matching blouses. Soon we were no longer quibbling over such an unimportant point. She was making her own decisions as well as learning to coordinate her outfits.

Insight for Parenting: Being allowed to make choices within certain limits was a happy step toward making more important decisions later.

Rabbit-Fur Coats

When putting coats on lay-away in July, the question of rabbit-fur coats came up. My eleven- and nine-year-olds had eyed these on their friends all last winter and were very desirous of having one themselves. I could not justify the extra expense until I thought of allowing them to raise or earn half the money for the coats. They eagerly accepted the challenge. Little did I realize how seriously they would work on this.

At the church picnic, because they were busy gathering everyone's aluminum cans to sell, their efforts came to the attention of many of our friends and they gave my girls real approval and encouragement. It became a project that built their self-esteem and enlarged their relationships with adult Christians in the church. They are now enjoying the benefits of their hard, diligent work—two beautiful rabbit-fur coats! One added benefit is that Mom and Dad ended up paying less on the coats than if *we* had picked out coats and paid the full amount!

Insight for Parenting: Thinking of a creative alternative to help these girls become involved in reaching their goals, gave them some practice in responsibility and built their self-esteem.

Do It Yourself

At the change of each season I always go through my children's clothes and have them try on their things to see what fits, what they've outgrown, what they have, and what they need. It also provides a time for cleaning out and straightening drawers and closets.

Last spring when I came to my twelve-year-old daughter's clothes, I was in a big hurry to get that job done and go on to something else. She was uncooperative. After each dress was either tried on or held up, she'd lie down and I'd have to prod her on. I found that some clothes were still wearable, but she had not worn them. When I asked why, her only answer was, "I don't know." I became upset and said, "It seems to me if I am willing to take my time, you at least ought to be willing to cooperate!" Finally, almost in tears, I left, saying, "You can just do it yourself!"

If I had been more sensitive to her needs, I would have realized that at twelve she wanted just that—to do it herself. She felt she was old enough to make the decisions on her own. She was also modest and did not want to be dressing and undressing in front of people.

Fortunately I realized my mistake and her need immediately after my exit. So I went back, apologized, and told her I loved her and appreciated the fact that she wanted to take charge of her own things. She finished up in no time!

Insight for Parenting: This mother recognized that needs and feelings changed as the child grew into adolescence and that her daughter wanted to be trusted to decide about her own clothes.

Cleat Club

Our ten-year-old son expressed a desire for cleats to use in the fall soccer season, even though not all the other children had them and they were not required equipment. I decided to see how much he wanted them by asking if he would be willing to "work" for them.

We formed a Cleat Club. It consisted of some selected biographies and other good books for him to read. With each book he read and gave a short report on, we put a penny for each page into a special "cleat" account. The club was begun several months before fall, so that there was plenty of time for the points to accumulate. Our being of limited means and his having large feet meant to me that the shoes may not come easily—no sales or thrift-shop buys! My son received his shoes before his first game and had even more points than actually needed.

Insight for Parenting: The Cleat Club not only provided incentive for good reading, but helped this boy have a responsible part in seeing this "want" supplied.

Library Fines

Our children are expected to pay their own library fines on overdue books. When one of our daughters was seven, she had an overdue book that required a "precious" quarter fee. Our new library had a slot on the outside for depositing books when the library was not open. So, thinking she would escape the fine, she put the overdue book in the slot when the library was open! I happened to size up the situation and asked her about it. When the truth came out, she had to go ask the librarian to get the book from the large container inside the slot, determine the amount owed, and pay the fine. We discussed the principle involved—honesty. To my knowledge, she has not had an overdue book since then—three years ago.

Insight for Parenting: Covering up a failure with a lie was not the way out. This wise mother helped her daughter face the issue and taught her one more lesson in honesty.

Anger Replaced by Trust

I had a problem with my two-year-old daughter writing on the walls. I became angry, kept the crayons hidden, and watched her all the time when she did have the crayons. This did not help at all! I decided it was time to build trust, so I cleaned off a special place to put her crayons and coloring books. The crayons were put in an open box, so she could go to them at any time and color in her coloring books. I reinforced in her mind what she already knew— that crayons were only for the coloring books, never for the walls.

Three months have passed and she has never marked the walls. I praise the Lord that anger has been replaced by trust.

Insight for Parenting: This mother trusted her two-year-old to take responsibility for the correct use of her crayons and was rewarded with obedience.

"I Nearly Choked!"

One day I went shopping for school clothes with our eighth-grader. Using money he had earned on his own he purchased a pair of shoes for seventy-five dollars. That was lots of money to us at the time. I nearly choked right there in the department store, but managed to keep silent. My thoughts were, *Just let him make his own decision with his own money. He'll find out the hard way that he was wrong!* Would you believe he wore those shoes almost every day the whole year and part of the next, and he took loving care of them without being told!

Long after the shoes were gone I told him my reaction to his choice, and we had a good time of sharing. I explained that I could see now he had made a wise decision and used good judgment. Parents aren't always right!

Insight for Parenting: Letting him choose and pay for his own shoes gave him a greater sense of responsibility to care for them and helped Mom see teenagers *can* make good choices.

Last One Home

When our teenagers have dates or go out for other activities in the evening, we write their names down on a specially prepared paper just inside the door. When they come home they cross their own name out. The last one home is then responsible to lock the door and turn off the lights.

Insight for Parenting: These parents, whose children have proved to be dependable, demonstrate their trust by this simple nightly routine.

Wonders for Self-Esteem

Time is such a precious commodity in our household, yet just as with love, if it is given away, it will be returned. My five-year-old daughter, Joy, wanted so badly to learn to help in the kitchen. We all know how much "help" a child that age is, so I kept putting her off. Finally, I set aside one afternoon to spend with her in the kitchen. As a result of that one solitary afternoon, Joy now makes her own breakfast and packs her own lunch. Not only has she become a real help and timesaver for me, but she feels so good about herself and proud of her skills. It has done wonders for her self-esteem.

Insight for Parenting: A few moments of time turned a bothersome preschooler into an asset to Mother and gave the child a good feeling about herself.

Family Powwow

When we were teenagers, each Sunday after church we had what we called our Family Powwow. We got our heads together and discussed what each of our schedules would be for the week. This helped us not to forget our family and become too independent as we all went our separate ways. We also learned consideration for others. If my youngest sister needed a ride somewhere, we would work out which one of us could take her. Or, if we had special jobs to do together we would plan for that. For example, we would figure out when we could all put in our hour of weeding and do it together. Instead of a drag, it would turn into a party.

Insight for Parenting: Simply by discussing the week ahead, these teenagers learned to consider others and take some responsibility for one another's needs.

A Limited Choice

There is always a problem of what clothes my children want to wear—usually the worst they own! We solved the problem by giving them a limited choice. In the mornings my six-year-old chooses from two pairs of jeans which I lay out. Then I ask if he wants a long- or short-sleeved shirt. I choose two from the drawer and he picks from these.

The solution with my three-year-old came after she and I cried for thirty minutes before kindergarten one day. She picks out the stay-at-home play clothes, I pick out the go-places clothes. Now our mornings run smoothly, and the children are still learning to make some choices.

Insight for Parenting: Limiting the possibilities of choice according to their age and ability gave the children satisfaction and brought peace to the morning.

What actions or attitudes have you noticed in your children that show they are making progress in becoming responsible persons?

His Own Decision

My boy thought he might like to join a club for boys. He visited one night and came back to tell us the boys were pretty rough. He didn't like their language and said, "I don't want to be a part of that!" I had thought this was true of the club, but was glad to see he was able to make his own decision not to join—and for good reasons.

Insight for Parenting: Based on what he had learned about right and wrong at home, this boy was able to make his own intelligent decision that the club didn't meet his standards.

Standing Alone

One of the kids in our oldest daughter's class brought a tape of rock music to play at recess. While all of the other kids were crowded around his desk listening to it, Becky stayed at her own desk.

"Chicken"

When the rest of the boys decided to "play chicken" and stay outside after the recess bell rang, Eldon went in and sat in his seat obediently, even though he was laughed at by the rest of the class. I am grateful that even at a young age he is willing to "stand alone" for right.

Overcome Lying

Our sixth-grader finds that most of the students in her school tell lies. She shared with us one evening on our way to church that she was trying so hard not to lie in any way because she knows it is sin. She expressed how she now realized that even exaggeration was a form of lying and that she had been praying for help to overcome this.

Insight for Parenting: Standing alone, when necessary, is one good indication that a child is taking steps toward responsibility.

Self-Control

While we were all discussing the dinner Sally had prepared from new recipes learned in cooking class, John (twelve) was courteous and quiet and ate the whole dinner. Later he confided to me that it was so overseasoned it burned his mouth. He knew how much it meant to his sister to prepare this dinner, and I was so pleased at the self-control he showed by not complaining.

Provoked to Anger

My youngest son has a big problem with his temper, and his older brother likes to pick on him to provoke him to anger. The other day he was starting to get angry when all of a sudden he said, "I am going to ask God to help me so I don't get mad." What a step toward responsibility for his own reactions!

The Stress Test

My little three-year-old loves to see how much stress plastic things can take before they break. He has broken many plastic ice cream spoons and thinks it's lots of fun. He knows plastic toys are not to be used for this "stress test," but one time the temptation was really great. While I was watching, I saw him slightly bending a little plastic car. He was going to bite on it next when he saw me watching from another room. I didn't say anything or give any expression of disapproval, but he stopped, thought a while, then came and hugged me. What a victory!

Insight for Parenting: Each of the children in these last three examples made progress in self-control at their own level of growth and ability. Ask, *Have I commended a child recently for evidence of self-control?*

Taking Her Place in the Family

Our oldest girl was told she would need to stay home and miss a basketball game to take care of a younger sister because of an emergency that called her father and me away. She simply said, "That's all right, I don't mind." A whole group of her friends were going to the game, but she didn't question us in any way. We were so pleased to see her take her place of responsibility in the family without complaint.

Insight for Parenting: Enjoying the benefits and accepting the responsibilities are both part of being in a family.

Sit There, Body!

From a young age we instructed our daughter that her body was to serve her, rather than become a dictator over her. As she practiced the piano, occasionally I overheard her say aloud, "You sit right here, body, even if you feel like running around, until I finish ten more minutes of piano!"

Insight for Parenting: Learning that her body and emotions didn't have to control her, gave this girl victory over more than piano practice.

"I'll Be the Winner"

Our college girl is living at home this month and practice teaching in our neighborhood grade school. She is working hard with her lesson plans. A good friend, who also teaches there, told her, "You are doing far more than is necessary for four hours credit." Debbie replied, "I may be, but I see this as an opportunity to learn and observe. I want the time to be worthwhile. I'll be the winner, even if I gain only four credits." I breathed a "thank You" to the Lord that our little Debbie had grown up!

Insight for Parenting: Doing more than was required to "get by" was a good indication that Debbie was assuming responsibility for making a success of her career.

What did your parents do which you consider a major help in making you a responsible person?

Start to Finish

The summer before my fifth grade I wanted a white zipper Bible. I promised my folks I would save my allowance all summer just to buy it. I really wanted that Bible.

About two weeks after my commitment, I had lost some enthusiasm and tried to talk my folks into letting me spend some of my money, but they wouldn't. I managed to survive and finally got my Bible. I was proud that with good parental influence I had "stuck by my guns" and achieved my goal. To this day, that was the best lesson in responsibility I have ever learned. When I start something, I know I must finish it. This has carried over into all areas of life, including paying my bills!

Insight for Parenting: Her parents' steady influence helped her keep her commitment, taught her a good life habit, and brought her great satisfaction.

Half and Half

When I was eight, my dad did something that developed a lot of patience in me. I expressed an interest in encyclopedias, so he sat down with me and explained, "These books cost a lot of money, but, Emily, if you are willing to save twenty cents out of every fifty cents of your allowance each week for a whole year, then you will pay for part and I will pay for part and you can have your own encyclopedias."

I did give up that part of my allowance, and a year later the books arrived. I can still remember the ecstatic joy I felt with them spread all over the living room! It was some years before I realized that they had cost more than twenty-dollars. I thought we had each paid half!

Insight for Parenting: Setting the goal, sticking to the agreement, and then seeing the fruit of her patience taught this eight-year-old more about practical living than all the "learning" found in the whole set of encyclopedias.

To Buy or Not to Buy

Instead of simply running out and buying a new item the family wanted or needed, my father always had us pray together about it. We had a list we would add to as we prayed: "How God Is Providing," or a second list of obvious ways we could see He was saying no to our request.

I so clearly remember how we prayed for a camera. My father was a minister and within ten days he had had four special services. The total amount he received was the exact cost of the camera.

Another time we prayed for a travel trailer for camp-outs. We got no leads, no money, poor weather, less interest by everyone in the family and we eventually dropped the whole idea.

Insight for Parenting: This wise father was helping his children place the right value on material things, as they let God provide and direct in their buying.

Shopping With Dad

When I was between nine and thirteen I went to town every Saturday with Dad. I had a list, and sometimes two, of weekly shopping items for the family. Dad would discuss with me the various things I was supposed to buy. He explained the difference between quality and quantity, how to do comparative shopping, and then gave me a chance to practice what I was learning.

By allowing me to do the family shopping, my folks gave me a good background in handling money. This is the only thing I can remember my dad teaching me, so such attention from Dad and the responsibility I had made me feel loved and useful. Unsurprisingly, this is one of the few areas in which I have self-confidence.

Insight for Parenting: Instruction followed by personal experience brought self-confidence, but the biggest benefit of the Saturday trip was the attention she got from Dad and the sense of love that attention communicated.

See It Through

I think one of the most effective things my parents did was to remind us that we weren't forced to accept outside responsibilities. However, once we did, it was our job to see it through and keep our commitment. They expected it; God expected it; and it wasn't long till we expected it of ourselves. If I promised a lady I'd baby-sit on Saturday night and later got a date invitation, I baby-sat! I ended up with a good feeling of a job well done!

Insight for Parenting: Expecting to keep commitments is one of the best habits a parent can pass on to a child.

Powerful Lessons in Economics

I wanted a bicycle so badly for Christmas. I asked for one and just expected it, never giving a thought to how my parents could buy it. On Christmas morning when I came downstairs, I saw standing in among the mountain of presents my "new" bike. Only it wasn't new. One look showed me my dad had painstakingly overhauled and repaired an old bike, even using aluminum paint for a chrome look.

It was my first and most powerful lesson in economics. I realized at that moment that I had asked for something they couldn't afford, but they had tried to do the best they could. I still cry when I think about it. It was the only time in my life that I ever felt my parents really loved me.

Insight for Parenting: The example of these parents taught you don't spend what you don't have; there may be other creative ways of getting what you need.

Contribution to the Family

When we were quite young, my parents started giving us responsibilities around the house each week. Mom kept a paper inside the cupboard that she changed each week. On it were each of our household responsibilities for the week—daily ones like bedroom, dishes, trash, and so on; Saturday ones with bigger, one-time jobs that varied with the season and needs. In retrospect I see that I had a sense of satisfaction when the jobs were completed and well done. I could tell a difference between me and my friends whose moms did everything for them. Their parents never seemed to need them, whereas my chores gave me the feeling that I was making a meaningful and appreciated contribution to the whole family.

Insight for Parenting: Children need to feel a part of the family, not only by receiving the benefits of love and provision, but by contributing to the household by becoming a part of the family "work force."

How do you feel your parents could have better helped you become a responsible person?

Trust

Maturity and responsibility took a long time to acquire because I was raised in an atmosphere of mistrust and perfectionism. I felt unloved and frustrated by never seeming to be able to do anything "right" according to my parents' standards. I felt they never trusted me to do a job, but were always looking over my shoulder to see if I was doing it their way. Therefore I adopted an attitude of futility—"What's the use"—and did only that which I was specifically instructed to do—no more, no less. A simple word of honest praise or encouragement would have meant so much.

More Supervision

I believe my parents could have helped me the most by providing more supervision in projects and ongoing activities. We would often become enthused about a project like raising an animal in 4-H. However, whatever I chose to do was always my project from beginning to end, and I never had any supervision to be sure it was properly carried through. It seldom was. The same was true of piano lessons. There was never a reminder or set time for practice, so eventually all would fall by the wayside. Something within me seemed to cry out for some rules, something to force me to follow through and feel good about a job completed.

No Excuses

I wish my parents would not have let me make excuses for my unacceptable actions or moods. I believe this would have helped me become a more responsible person.

Insight for Parenting: Ask, *Are any of my children silently crying out for supervision, controls, acceptance, and trust?*

Jobs to Do

I wish my parents had given me definite tasks and responsibilities around the house. I used piano practicing and studying as excuses for not doing the few jobs I *was* assigned. My mother was a very efficient homemaker who could do these things much more quickly and better than I, so rather than force me to do them, she did them herself. The result? Housework and cooking were a big shock and a tremendous adjustment to me when I was first married. I had a great deal to learn at twenty-four that I should have learned at twelve.

Insight for Parenting: Giving a child definite jobs around the house makes him an integral and useful member of the family and prepares him for life's future demands.

Share Expenses

One thing I think my parents should have done was to make me help with grocery and other household expenses while I was living at home and working. I lived at home until I was twenty-three and made pretty good money, but they never asked for a cent and I never gave them one. I feel guilty about it now.

Insight for Parenting: Assuming her fair share of household expenses would have made this girl feel good about taking her place in the adult world.

As you look back, how do you feel you could have better taught your children responsibility?

Unhealthy Dependence

I was sure my family needed my organizational skills. I enjoyed giving directions: the best way to dress, the most profitable way to study, the most interesting places to visit. The list went on and on. Unfortunately it did not help them. Instead it encouraged an unhealthy dependence on me.

Eventually I realized that as long as I was willing to make the decisions, they were being denied practice in cultivating that skill. With much difficulty on my part I gave them less direction and found, joyfully, that the less direction I gave the more willingly they made choices.

Too Fussy

I was in too much of a hurry and too fussy. I wanted everything to be done "just so" and "right now" so I did it myself. I wish now I had let the children do more and been less fussy about the results. Because I did everything for them, they did not need to be responsible.

More Than Surface

I have been an authoritarian with my children. I gave an order and it had better be done—my way, in my time, and with no discussion! For example, I wanted the rooms to be clean before school so I yelled, criticized, and threatened to get results. The results I got were resentment, rebellion, and sneakiness. The rooms may have looked neat on the surface but clothes, food, collectibles—everything—were hidden under the bed, stashed in the closet, or stuffed into drawers. It will only be God changing my attitude that will heal this situation so my children will realize it's more than the surface that matters.

Freedom to Choose

I wish I had given my oldest son more freedom to make his own choices and not been so strict with him on trivial matters. He now finds it difficult to make up his own mind on even small things. I should have "cut the cord" sooner, trusted God more, and allowed him to make his own mistakes earlier in life.

Insight for Parenting: Ask, *Do any of these examples warn me that I'm leaning too heavily in one direction—too fussy, too much direction, too protective, too authoritarian? The key is balance.*

7

Learning From Our Parents and Our Children

"You, therefore who teach another, do you not teach yourself?"

Romans 2:21

And so we come to the blessed but solemn truth: Let parents be what they want their children to be. Let Father and Mother lead a life marked by love to God and man; this is the atmosphere in which loving children can be trained. Let all the dealings with the children be in holy love. Cross words, sharp reproof, impatient answers are infectious. Love demands and fears not self-sacrifice; time and thoughtful attention and patient perseverance are needed to train our children aright. When our children hear us speak of others, of friends or enemies, of the low, the vulgar, the wicked, let the impression be the love of Christ we seek to show. In all the communication of Father and Mother with each other, let mutual esteem and respect, tender considerateness and willing self-forgetfulness prove to the children that love is possible and blessed.

> Andrew Murray
> in *How to Raise Your Children for Christ*

What have you learned from your parents?

She Begged Forgiveness

My mother entrusted me with a check for a large sum of money for some kind of school expense. At school, when I reached into my purse—no check! I came home after school and confessed I didn't have the money. Mother immediately concluded I had lost it and severely disciplined me in spite of my pleas of innocence.

The next day Mother discovered the money on top of the refrigerator! I had not even picked it up from the kitchen table to take to school and Mother had absentmindedly picked it up and placed it on top of the refrigerator (a favorite place for loose papers to check through later).

On her knees, with such sobbing, my mother apologized and begged for my forgiveness. I'll never forget that. It has made me able to say, "Forgive me," even to my three-year-old son.

Spanking Was a Three-Day Ordeal

In being disciplined as a child I don't think I ever sensed forgiveness for my wrongs. After getting a spanking it was a two- or three-day ordeal for relations to get back to normal between Mom and me. It was as though I had to keep paying for my wrong and then in two or three days it would all blow over. My reaction to life now is to keep trying to justify my wrong. I've also learned to carry a grudge, or in other words to carry on this unforgiving attitude.

I discovered this one day at school when one of my pupils got a spanking. He had paid for his bad behavior and now he had a clean slate and needed acceptance. I felt compelled to keep on condemning even though I knew I shouldn't. It took Jesus' love in me to be anything more than polite to the child. I had to do a lot of thinking and praying about this attitude in me.

On Time or a Little Early

I learned to be responsible by parental example. One big lesson I learned was to be on time or a little early wherever I went. My father had not only verbally told me this, but actually made sure I got to places on time. I didn't realize I had picked up this trait until I got to college and discovered there were people who seemed to be late for everything. I am always ten to fifteen minutes early and it's a good feeling.

Insight for Parenting: Thinking reflectively over the good and bad things you remember from your childhood is one effective way of learning how to parent.

What good things do you think your children have learned from your example?

Courtesy and Respect

Please and *thank you* have always been words my husband and I use regularly—for two reasons: common courtesy and respect. We treat our children in the same way. The result is that "please" and "thank you" are natural conditioned responses from Jim and Barbara. Usually we don't even have to remind them or make an issue of their remembering.

Every Monday Morning

All my married life I have written to my mother and my mother-in-law every Monday morning before I started the week doing anything else. My daugher, Jill, saw me do this all the years she lived at home. Now, since she has a home of her own, she writes to me each week. I feel the example I put before her is the reason she is so faithful in writing to me.

Substitute Something Positive

When we have to say no to one of our children, whenever possible we like to substitute it with something positive that they *can* do. The other day I noticed that our seven-year-old son had caught on to this. His eighteen-month-old brother wanted to play with an intercom. When Marvin saw that his little brother was unhappy because we said no to his playing with the intercom, Marvin got a little piece of cardboard, drew a picture of the intercom, and handed it to his little brother. Peter loved it and played with it for days, and we commended Marvin for his thoughtfulness.

"I See a Monster"

One night after the two older children had already gone into the house, I was having trouble getting the two-year-old to get out of the car. "I see a monster over there," she exclaimed. "No, there is no monster, and besides, Jesus always watches us and protects us." I pointed to the stars,

"He made all those beautiful stars and He can take care of us."

I didn't know how much sank into her young mind and heart until later that night I heard her cooing to her doll, "Don't be afraid, Jesus loves you, look at all those stars!"

"That's Okay, Randy"

When our three-year-old was carrying a loaf of bread outside for lunch, he had it open-side down and the bread fell out. Kathy (eight years old) started picking it up and said, "That's okay, Randy. It was an accident. You were helping." It had been our practice not to make an issue of accidents and now she was following our example.

"Have You Tried Praying?"

My sister-in-law was telling me about a problem. When she had finished I asked her if I could pray for her. She agreed that we could pray about it, so I read two verses from the Bible—Matthew 21:22 and John 15:7. Then I told her how God had answered some specific prayers for me.

My son was sitting in the other room when all of this was happening. About two months later he had a friend over after school. I overheard him saying to his friend, "Have you ever tried praying to God so that He will help you with your problems?" I was a pretty proud mother at that moment.

No "Flipping Out"

By watching the way I have learned to accept accidents around the house (calmly and without "flipping out") my children are learning to accept accidents calmly too.

Insight for Parenting: Encourage yourself by noticing the good things you've passed on to your children.

What bad habits do you think your children have learned from your example?

One of Those "Sunday Headaches"

One Sunday afternoon I overheard my daughter saying, "I guess I have one of those Sunday headaches." I recognized the phrase. She had heard me say this again and again after working with four-year-olds all Sunday morning. I never realized how negative it sounded until I heard it from a six-year-old.

"All You Do Is Criticize"

Our oldest daughter, sixteen, and her brother, fifteen, were making pizza. Her brother was not an experienced pizza baker. Lisa sounded just like me, "What are you doing now? That's not the right way. Look at the mess you're making!" After listening for a while, brother said to his sister, "All you do is criticize me," and I was remembering how many times I had said those same critical words to Lisa.

"Come On, You Dumb Car"

Our ten-year-old car was getting a little hard to start. One day when I was in a hurry and couldn't get the car started, I sat behind the wheel saying, "Come on, you dumb car." A few days later, I tried to start the car and it was its good old self—it wouldn't start. From the backseat a small voice with a very familiar tone to it piped up with, "Come on, you dumb car! It sure is a dumb car, right, Mom?"

"Sit Up ... Elbows Off ..."

I am a nag at the dinner table about table manners. "Sit up to the table!" "Chew with your mouth closed!" "Don't talk with your mouth full!" "Keep your elbows off the table!" "Don't pile your plate so full—you may have seconds." As a result I hear my thirteen-year-old son use these same words to nag his younger brothers.

"Don't Touch Me!"

When I got upset with my husband and he would come near me to try to patch things up, I would shout, "Don't touch me." One day when our five-year-old got upset with us and we started to come near to her to talk to her, she pulled away defiantly and said, "Don't touch me!" She kept this up until I stopped responding this way to my husband.

"So What!"

My son, Ken, is at the age where he copies everything his dad and I say. There were two little words I had been saying lately. I would say something like, "Ken, let's go get the mail." "But, Mom, it's windy." "*So what*, let's go anyway." Now those two little words were coming back to us. "Ken, you didn't put my books back where you got them." "*So what!*" Oh, how disrespectful they sounded! That wasn't the way I meant them, but it sure drove home the point—children are great imitators; be careful what you give them to imitate.

Monkey Hear, Monkey Say

Our four-year-old is just at the age of "monkey see, monkey do" and "monkey hear, monkey say." I have always had a habit of indulging in "pet sayings" such as *good*

grief, this is ridiculous, rats. Often I hear Jason saying these
very same words while playing or talking with other children. It has recently occurred to me how meaningless these
clichés sound when I use them habitually, but how unbe-
coming they sounded when coming from a four-year-old.

Insight for Parenting: Children are great imitators—it's
one key way God plans for them to learn. You can
learn volumes about yourself by being alert to their
little echoes of your words and actions.

What have you learned by listening to or watching your children?

"How Did You Learn?"

One day I was making cream puffs and my four-year-old
daughter wanted to help. I told her, "No, I have to do this
project myself." She started asking questions as only four-
year-olds can, "How did you learn to make cream puffs?" I
told her I had to go to cooking school to learn how to cook,
because my mommy would never let me . . . cook in her
kitchen. . . .

Before I finished the sentence I realized what I had just
said and what I was doing. Visions of my little girl going to
cooking school to learn what I could now have the joy of
teaching her flashed through my mind. I thanked God out
loud for showing me my mistake, pulled up a stool for her
to stand on, and said, "Here, Sara, you can help me stir the
batter."

Quiet Enough to Listen

One evening when I was sick in bed, one of our boys
came into the room and told me some things he had never

talked to me about before. I have forgotten the details, but I remember asking, "Why haven't you talked with me about these things before?" To which he replied in a very sincere, quiet tone, "Well, Mother, I guess this is the first time I ever caught you still and quiet long enough to listen." After that experience I certainly tried to give more time and attention to my children and not make them wait till I'm sick in bed.

"Don't You Love Your Baby?"

As I was watching my two little girls at play, I began to realize something about myself. They were playing house. One was the mother and one was the baby. The oldest was constantly getting on to the "baby" for just about everything. Finally I asked her, "Don't you love your baby?" She looked at me in surprise and said, "Well sure, if I didn't I wouldn't care how she grew up." Well, that was a familiar phrase! I realized how I had overdone a good thing and reminded her a few too many times that we corrected her because we loved her.

I Saw Myself in Action

One day I got very angry at my teenage daughter and let her have a barrage of yelling and harsh words. My little granddaughter, age three, was watching the whole unhappy episode. When her grandfather came home, she met him at the door with, "Candy got into trouble and Grandmother said. . . ." Whereupon she went through the whole episode word for word including all my gestures. I really saw myself "in action" and was ashamed.

Spanks With a Frown

I notice that our three-year-old spanks his Jack doll with an angry frown more than he cuddles and "loves" him. I feel he thinks the main job of mothers or fathers is to spank. I hope by showing more patience and love toward him, I can see his love come out, even to his toys.

Bossy Manner

If a mother wonders how she sounds to her children she need only listen as her daughter talks to her dolls or her pets. When I first realized this, my reaction was, "No, she must have heard that somewhere else," but then I finally admitted that she learned her bossy manner with her dolls from me. How ashamed I was. I realized then how much I needed to change my manner.

Playing Their Roles

One day we observed our three older children playing house and were pleasantly pleased with the way they played their roles. When "Daddy" (eight-year-old Josh) came home, "Mommy" (seven-year-old Mary), and "daughter" (four-year-old Sara) ran to the door to greet him. Then they had a pleasant meal, sat around and played games together, and then read the Bible. If this is their impression of family life, then we must have done something right.

More Emphasis on Inner Beauty

This morning my daughter came to me and asked what clothes she should wear to school. There wasn't much choice since the laundry had piled up over the weekend, but I laid out some pants and a blouse. She looked at my selection and insisted they didn't match. I told her they looked fine to me, but since her opinion differed from mine, perhaps she could select something else.

In the meantime, her father, who had overheard the whole incident, came to me and said, "Where did she ever learn to be so fussy about her clothes?" I just smiled, but I knew she was only following my example. I decided it was time to put less emphasis on clothes and more emphasis on inner beauty.

"You're Judgmental!"

Recently I mentioned to our fifteen-year-old son before he left for school that it might be wise for me to read the book he had brought home from the library. He immediately became defensive and said, "You're always checking up on me! If you'd like to know it, you're judgmental!"

My first instinct was to tell him off, but since I'd been to the Workshop last winter, I asked the Lord just to help me not to hurt him. So I answered, "You're right, Andy. I *am* judgmental and it wasn't easy for you to tell me. I'm going to ask you to pray for me in my weakness, because the last thing I'd want to do is discourage you in your Christian life. No doubt you're growing faster than your mother."

He left for school in tears, but upon returning in the evening, he sat down to chat. It wasn't long before he said, "Mom, I'm sorry about this morning." I responded in love and all was well again.

After a while the right time came to discuss the fact that his father and I are answerable to God for what he sees, hears, and puts into his mind and that we want to help him learn to choose the right books. He was ready to show us the library book, and it was a good time to discuss standards for reading material and how *he* can discern the good and bad.

"Mommy, You Need a Song"

I have tried to encourage singing and praising in our home—especially when things were not going well or when everyone seemed to be having a bad day. One day we were driving in the car and I was very rushed and irritable. My little boy looked over at me and said, "Mommy, I think you need a song!" So we all sang and had a much better day.

Also, the boys enjoy children's records and we play them frequently. One deals with the fruit of the Spirit. One day while driving I said something in a rather unpleasant way to the driver in front of me. My little boys piped up, "Mom, you're not being patient like Herbert!" (Herbert is a snail on the record teaching patience.) So all of us are learning patience and song.

The Anger Showed

I corrected my daughter one time for something very minor, but I was very angry when I did it. I thought the incident was forgotten, but several hours later she was acting very odd. When I asked her what was the matter she said, "You're still angry with me, Mother." I said, "No, Lucy, I'm not angry. I have forgiven you." Her probing question was, "How come your face is still angry?"

Insight for Parenting: Listening to and watching your children helps you know what you are communicating to them. It may also reveal to you your manner, a blind spot in your mothering, or an overemphasis on one phase of training that you could correct.

What helpful responses did you get when you asked your children, "How can I improve as a mother?"

You're Too Busy

It occurred to me that my relationship with my teenage daughter was cooling off and there was certainly a generation gap showing. When I asked her where I could improve, her reply was as follows:

"Mother, you could stop screaming commands at me. You could talk *to* me, not *at* me. If I suggest anything we could do together, you either veto it or you are too busy with your own pet projects. If I get high marks at school you don't praise me, you say, 'You were just lucky.' I know you don't want me to get stuck up, but praise is appreciated sometimes. Mother, I do have certain interests, but you don't seem to be interested in what I am doing."

This was quite a revelation to me. When I sat down and began to think things over, and to ask God to show me, I realized I did scream at her sometimes, especially when I was tired. And I *was* much too involved in clubs and various civic affairs to give her the time she needed for quiet talks.

After thinking these things through I began to give up some of my offices in civic affairs and to devote time to her and to her interests. I tried not to scream at her, and I praised her when she stood second in her class. Above all I had to ask her to forgive me for my faults. Our relationship began to improve and warm up, as we worked to understand each other better because of this confrontation.

Insight for Parenting: By studying the responses of children to the question, "How can Mother improve?" we can often discover what causes hurts, misunderstandings, and breakdowns in communication between parents and children. Ask the Lord to make you sensitive to anything He wants to teach you as you read the following answers to the question, "How can Mother improve?"

Praise Me More

My oldest daughter, sixteen, suggested:

1. Maybe you could praise me more. If you like the way something looks on me or the way I do something, tell me. If you let me know what you like about me, I'll be able to accept criticism better.

2. Sew a lot!

3. Always be ready to listen, but if I'm not ready to talk, don't press it. That doesn't help any.

4. Don't compare me with other people.

5. Buy me a typewriter so I can improve my typing. That's all I can think of now. You don't need to ask me about them now though. Think about them for a while first. Also, no matter what, always keep sharing stuff with me and tell me new stuff you've learned.

Say It Once

I had hardly finished asking the question when my son, age thirteen, said, "Yes, Mom, you shouldn't tell me things over and over so many times—it's being crabby." It was a good suggestion and he's responding just as well to being asked *once*, rather than impatiently reminded several times. I'm also learning 1 Corinthians 13 to remind me that love is patient and kind.

Use Fewer Words

My college son replied, "Mom, you talk too much. If you would give your advice or reprimand in fewer words it would be more effective. When you keep talking, I just quit listening." As I have tried to be more brief, definite, and to the point, his reactions are much better.

If You Promise, Do It

Our married daughter said, "Mother, so often you say you're going to do a certain thing but you fail to follow through on it." I know this has caused her frustration and sadness through the years. For example, I often made the comment that when she had her first baby I would be there to help care for them when she came home from the hospital.

When the event took place, she was living 150 miles away. A few weeks before delivery I began to have doubts about whether I should go. My husband would be alone and I reasoned, "He needs me in the business."

My daughter said, "I have had plenty of help offered, so don't worry about coming." Actually she was only being brave so as not to let me know how hurt she really was. My daughter's suggestion was: "Mother, don't say you're going to do thus and so. Rather say, I'll *try*, but won't promise."

You Can Still Worry

My daughter made this list:
1. Your temper.

2. Making us play the piano sometimes in front of company.

3. Making me embarrassed in front of my friends.

4. You worry too much! You can still worry. Don't forget worrying completely, <u>PLEASE!</u>

She evidently thinks worrying is very dear to my heart and doesn't want to deprive me of it completely! It makes it quite obvious what I need to work on.

Sit Back on Your Chair

Vicky answered, "Mom, when you play table games with us, please sit back on your chair." I realized that when I join them for games, I always sit on the edge of my chair, as though I may have to leave any minute. She wants to feel I'm going to stay to the finish.

Don't Interfere

Our independent fourteen-year-old son made the following carefully thought out list:

1. Don't be overprotective—for example, if I want to go swimming in the creek, don't worry so much about the holes.

2. Don't give me so much advice on how I should spend the money I earn.

3. Don't interrogate me about every detail of my life. For example, when I came home from a Sunday school picnic, you wanted to know everything I ate and did.

4. When Daddy and I are making a decision together, don't interfere.

5. When a group of my friends are here, and I ask permission to do something with them, don't make such an issue about it in the presence of the other boys.

Smile More

My daughter remarked, "Smile more, Mommy. Look as if you are happy." After the second or third admonition, I began to give some real thought and attention to her comments. I reached the conclusion that I was so engrossed in getting my "Mother-job" done that I was failing to express joy and love.

Listen to Me

The thing one daughter wanted most was for me to listen to her when she wanted to talk. I concentrated on this. Every time she talked to me I was very careful to give her my complete attention. Several months later she was complaining how terribly her older brother and sister treat her, "They never listen to me or pay any attention to me. Mom, you're the only one who listens to me when I talk." I took this as a victory and gave thanks to the Lord!

More Family Time

Each of my five children answered:

Child #1: Cook better meals.

Child #2: Be more strict. Spend more time on family outings. Be more sympathetic.

Child #3: Spend more time together as a family on outings. Be less stubborn.

Child #4: Spend more time on family outings.

Child #5: Pack better school lunches. Spend more time as a family. Buy me more pants.

Since four out of five asked for more family outings, that message came through loud and clear.

Pet Names

My daughter asked us to quit calling her names such as "Monkey," "Pumpkin," or other little pet names. The words were fine, she said, but our tone of voice when we used them conveyed displeasure and disapproval and it made her feel bad. We didn't realize we only used those names for correction. We honored her request and now do not use any name except hers in a nice tone of voice. It has been one link in the bridge back to a better relationship.

Get More Rest

My eight-year-old's list included:
1. Play with us more.
2. Do more jigsaw puzzles.
3. Teach me to "crowshay."
4. Get more rest.
5. Don't be so fussy.
6. Have more special dinners.

I'm already working on the "more rest," but this list also shows me a real need to spend more time just playing. I'm making a conscious effort to play with them each evening and both our six- and eight-year-olds love it. Today I am also going to teach her how to crochet.

Afraid of My Response

My daughter told me, "Mom, you make sure everyone knows when you're not feeling well or when you're in a bad mood." Now I see that in doing this, I set the whole family on edge and they stay away from me, fearful of my responses.

Some one-line answers to the question, "How can I improve as a mother?"

Let me do some big cleaning jobs like scrubbing the floor (ten years old).

You talk on the telephone too much.

Give us more freedom. Trust us more.

Don't blame me for everything because I'm the oldest.

Don't say cute things in front of my boyfriends.

Don't do *our* work; do your work only.